Tyrina Quinn Mobile Notary Service

The Ultimate Success Of Your Company Depends On Your Effort!

Starting your own company can be a lot of work, but it comes with great benefits. You create your own schedule, services provided, fees, and overall success.

This book is brought to you by the founder and CEO of
Tyrina Quinn Mobile Notary Service.

As a former realtor, who is now a successful Notary Public and Certified Signing Agent, the advice within these pages is based off both knowledge and experience.

Hopefully, this book will provide you with all the tools you will need to start your own mobile notary company.

Best Wishes,
Tyrina Quinn

ii

Mobile Notary Basics

By

Tyrina Quinn

This publication is designed to provide comprehensive information in regards to
the content covered and should not be construed as legal advice. If professional
assistance is required, the services of a competent professional person should be
sought.

DEDICATION

This book is dedicated to all the future Notaries.
May your success as a Notary Public be great and may
your business continue to flourish!

TABLE OF CONTENTS

SAMPLE DOCUMENTS

GLOSSARY OF TERMS

ACKNOWLEDGMENTS

I would like to thank those who helped me in my career as a Realtor. A special thank you, to my Office Manager for assisting me in Open Houses and to the Title Representatives who provided excellent training and customer service. I would especially like to thank my past and future clients for choosing Tyrina Quinn Mobile Notary Service as your Notary Public.

CHAPTER ONE

BECOMING A
NOTARY PUBLIC

CHAPTER 1
BECOMING A NOTARY PUBLIC

Notaries are sworn public servants for the State in which they reside in. As a Public Officer, appointed by the Secretary of State, the sole purpose of a Notary Public is to be an official witness to the execution of important documents. It is the job of the Notary Public to verify and confirm the identity of the individual signing the document.

As a Notary Public, you can witness the signing of various loan documents, Deeds of Trust, Powers of Attorney, and more. It is because of the importance of these documents that a Notary Public is to be a sworn public servant, requiring a background check and to be fingerprinted.

Convicted felons cannot become commissioned as a Notary Public. Notaries are entrusted with confidential information and often are required to facilitate the transfer of earnest money deposits from the client to the company, when completing loan document signings.

Some states require notaries to be bonded and some require them to have Errors and Omission Insurance as well, just in case the notary is found negligent in his or her job duties. It is very important when deciding to become a Notary Public that you are ready to take on the extensive responsibility that is required of a Sworn Public Servant.

The most important responsibility of a Notary Public is to certify the identity of the signer of the document. A Notary Public can use various forms of I.D. to verify the persons identity, such as a Government issued Driver License, Identification Card, Military I.D., or a valid Passport to verify the individual's identity, just to name a few.

A Notary Public also has the authority to administer oaths. However, a notary cannot prepare legal documents, such as immigration papers, or provide legal advice.

A Notary Public is required to keep a journal documenting every oath, affirmation, confirmation, or witnessing at which they preside over. The Journal is to remain a matter of public record and to be kept secured at all times. It is the responsibility of the Notary Public to make sure the journal is complete and accurate after each signing. When the notary public resigns or the journal is complete, the journal must be sent to the county in which the notary is registered.

A Notary Public must be bonded prior to appointment. As a public official, the bond helps the State receive reimbursement for their loss if the notary is found negligent of their duties. The bond also helps the client receive swift reimbursement by the company in which the notary public is bonded through. However, the notary public is still responsible to pay the fees or fines back.

Errors and Omission Insurance can also be purchased to aid the notary public in repaying the fines.

Each State has its own set of requirements for becoming a Notary Public. The process can take up to six weeks and a notaries term lasts for four years in most States. A Three-hour refresher course is required thirty to ninety days prior to the expiration of your commission to renew your term.

In order to be a Notary Public in the state of California you must be 18 years of age or older and a legal State resident. You must be able to speak, read, and write fluent English.

Some States require a six-hour course. There are also online courses that are offered. Once you take the six-hour course and take the exam, your test results will take 2-3weeks.

When you pass the exam, you will receive a package

from the Secretary of State with a list of places to get fingerprinted. Once your fingerprints are cleared, you will receive another package that will include a list of approved places for you to get bonded.

The packet will also have instructions on what to do to receive your Notary Public Commission. You will have 30 days to complete the instructions, so you will want to stay on top of everything. If it is not completed within the thirty days, you will have to restart the process from the beginning.

One of the instructions will be to take the Oath of Office at the County Recorder Office within the County you reside in and or conduct business in. Just because you take an Oath in the following County does not mean that you cannot conduct business in another County. You can conduct business anywhere throughout the State in which you reside in.

Once you receive your commission you can order your seal, your notary journal, thumb print inkpad, and other notarial supplies. You may want to purchase Jurat and Acknowledgement pads, or print them offline from the Secretary of State website free of charge.

You can also refer to your Secretary of State website for rules, guidelines and a Notary Public Handbook for additional training or questions.

Once commissioned, you can go to your local County Clerks or Recorder Office and choose a fictitious business name. A fictitious business name grants you the exclusive right to use and own your business name.

A fictitious business name not only allows you the right to protect your business name, it will also help you in the expansion of your services and products down the line. It allows you the opportunity to open up a business account and to accept checks or credit card payments. Having a fictitious business name signifies to clients that you are an official and professional business.

The process for applying for a fictitious business name is fairly simple. Once you choose a business name you must confirm that it is not already taken. The business name must be filed at your local County Clerk or Recorder Office for a fee. The County Clerk or Recorder Office will then give you the documents you will need to open up a bank account and to show proof of your business. You must also place a notice of filing in a local newspaper for four weeks, within thirty days of filing a fictitious business name.

Opening up a business account has many benefits. With a business account you are at an advantage of receiving special discounts and promotions from your financial institution. It also allows you to qualify to receive business credit cards with lower interest rates, purely for business transactions and related expenses.

Having a business account indicates that you are a credible business, allowing you to gain the business of even more companies. It will also help you keep a record of your transactions and business finances. The business account should be used solely for business purposes, which will come in handy during income tax time.

The benefits of becoming a Mobile Notary Service, is choosing your own hours. You can work full-time or part-time. Most importantly, you are your own boss. You decide what transactions or locations you want to service. It can be a side job or your only source of income.

A notary public can specialize in loan signings and or general notary work. Loan signings require the notarization of real estate transactions. General Notary Work consists of the notarization of sensitive documents for the general public, such as medical release forms, guardianship forms, and etc.

Whatever your own personal reason is for becoming a Notary Public, it's up to you to decide what level you want to take your business to.

NOTARY PUBLIC COMMISSION STATE REGUIRMENTS

ALABAMA
APPLICANT MUST:
- Be appointed and commissioned by the probate judges of the various counties.

ALASKA
APPLICANT MUST:
- Be 18 years of age or older.
- Be a legal resident of Alaska who is residing legally in the U.S.
- Applicants may not within 10 years before the commission takes effect have been convicted of a felony or incarcerated for a felony conviction.

ARIZONA
APPLICANT MUST:
- Be an Arizona resident.
- Be at least 18 years old.
- Not have been convicted of a felony unless your civil rights have been restored.

ARKANSAS
APPLICANT MUST:
- Be a legal resident of Arkansas or a legal resident of an adjoining state and employed in Arkansas.
- Be a United States citizen or a permanent resident alien.

- Be at least 18 years old.
- Be able to read and write English.
- Not have had Notary Commission revoked in the past 10 years.

CALIFORNIA
APPLICANT MUST:
- Be a legal resident of the State of California.
- Be 18 years of age.
- Satisfactorily complete a course of study approved by the Secretary of State.
- Pass a written examination prescribed by the Secretary of State.
- Pass a background check.

COLORADO
APPLICANT MUST:
- Be a resident of Colorado.
- Be at least 18 years old.
- Be able to read and write the English language.
- Be familiar with the Colorado Notary Law.
- Not have been convicted of a misdemeanor involving dishonesty, during the last five years.
- Not have had a felony conviction in your lifetime.
- Never have had a Notary Commission revoked.

CONNECTICUT
APPLICANT MUST:
- Be 18 years of age or older.

- Reside in, or have a principal place of business in Connecticut.
- Pass a written examination administered by the Secretary of the State's office.

DELAWARE
APPLICANT MUST:
- Be at least 18 years of age.
- Have a good character and reputation.
- Have a reasonable need for a Notary Commission.
- Have a legal residence including street address of the Notary within the State.

FLORIDA
APPLICANT MUST:
- Be at least 18 years of age and a legal resident of Florida.
- First-time applicants must submit proof that, within 1 year prior to the application, the applicant completed at least 3 hours of interactive or classroom instruction, including electronic notarization, and covering the duties of a Notary Public.

GEORGIA
APPLICANT MUST:
*Notaries receive their Commission from the Clerk of Superior Court within the County in which the Notary resides. *
- Be at least 18 years old.
- Be a citizen of the United States or a legal

resident of the United States.
- Be a legal resident of the County in which he or she applies.
- Have, and provide at the time of application, the applicant's operating telephone number.
- Be able to read and write English.

HAWAII
APPLICANT MUST:
- Be a United States citizen, or a national or permanent resident alien of the U.S., who diligently seeks citizenship upon becoming eligible to apply for U.S. citizenship.
- Be a Hawaii resident.
- Be at least 18 years old.
- Pass a written exam.

IDAHO
APPLICANT MUST:
- Be at least 18 years old.
- Be a resident of or employed in the State of Idaho.
- Be able to read or write the English language.
- Not have been removed from office for misconduct nor convicted of a serious crime within the last 10 years.

ILLINOIS
APPLICANT MUST:
- Be a citizen of the United States or an alien lawfully admitted for permanent residence.

- Be a resident of the State of Illinois for at least 30 days.
- Be at least 18 years of age.
- Be able to read and write the English language.
- Have not been convicted of a felony.
- Not have had a Notary Commission revoked during the past 10 years.

INDIANA
APPLICANT MUST:
- Be at least 18 years of age.
- Be a legal resident of the State of Indiana.

IOWA
APPLICANT MUST:
- Be at least 18 years of age.
- Be a citizen or permanent legal resident of the United States.
- Be a resident of or have a place of employment or practice in this State.
- Be able to read and write English.

KANSAS
APPLICANT MUST:
- Be a citizen of the United States.
- Be at least 18 years of age.
- Be a resident of this State, or a resident of a State bordering on this State and regularly carries on a business or profession in this State or is regularly employed in this State.

KENTUCKY
APPLICANT MUST:

- Be 18 years of age.
- Be a resident of or principally employed in the County from which he/she makes application.
- Be of good moral character.
- Be capable of discharging the duties imposed upon him/her by law.

LOUISIANA
APPLICANT MUST:

- Be a resident citizen or alien of this State.
- Be 18 years of age or older.
- Read, write, speak, and be sufficiently knowledgeable of the English language.
- Have received a high school diploma, have received a diploma for completion of a home study program approved by the State Board of Elementary and Secondary Education, or have been issued a high school equivalency diploma after successfully completing the test of General Educational Development.
- Not under interdiction or incapable of serving as a Notary because of mental infirmity.
- Have not been convicted of a felony, or if convicted of a felony, have been pardoned.
- Meet the requirements established by law for each commission sought.

MAINE
APPLICANT MUST:

- Be an adult resident of Maine (an adult is

defined as any person who has attained the age of 18).

- Be worthy of the public's trust.
- Have not been convicted of a crime for which imprisonment may be a penalty.
- Not be eligible for appointment while on bail, incarcerated, under probation or parole.
- Not be eligible for appointment for five years following the date of release from incarceration or termination of probation or parole, whichever comes last.

MARYLAND
APPLICANT MUST:
- Be at least 18 years of age.
- Be of known good character, integrity and abilities.
- Be living or working in the State of Maryland.

MASSACHUSETTS
APPLICANT MUST:
- Be at least 18 years of age.
- Reside legally or conduct business on a regular basis within Massachusetts.

MICHIGAN
APPLICANT MUST:
- Be at least 18 years old.
- Be a Michigan resident or maintain a place of business in Michigan.
- Be a U.S. citizen or possess proof of legal presence.

- Be a resident of the County in which the request appointment (if you do not reside in Michigan, maintain a principal place of business in the County of request appointment).
- Read and write in the English language.
- Be free of felony convictions within the past 10 years.
- Have not been convicted of 2 or more misdemeanor offenses involving a violation of the Michigan Notary Public Act within a 12-month period while commissioned or 3 or more misdemeanor offenses involving a violation of this Act within a 5-year period regardless of being commissioned.
- Not be currently serving a term of imprisonment in any state, county or federal correctional facility.

MINNESOTA
APPLICANT MUST:
- Not have held a previous commission that has expired.
- Be at least 18 years of age.
- Be either a Minnesota resident or a resident of a County in Iowa, North Dakota, South Dakota, or Wisconsin and list the Minnesota County he or she will be filing in upon receiving their commission.

MISSISSIPPI
APPLICANT MUST:
- Be at least 18 years of age or older.
- Be a resident of the State of Mississippi and have resided in the County of residence for at least 30 days prior to the submission of the application.
- Be a citizen or legal resident of the United States.
- Read and write English.
- Not be convicted of a felony.

MISSOURI
APPLICANT MUST:
- Be at least 18 years of age.
- Be a registered voter of the County within and for which he is commissioned or a resident alien of the United States.
- Be able to read and write the English language.
- Not have had his commission revoked during the past 10 years.

NEW JERSEY
APPLICANT MUST:
- Be a resident of New Jersey or a resident of an adjoining State who maintains, or is regularly employed in, an office in this State.
- Be 18 years or older.
- Not have been convicted of a crime under the laws of any State or the United States, for an offense involving dishonesty, or a crime of the first or second degree.

NEW MEXICO
APPLICANT MUST:

- Be a resident of New Mexico.
- Be at least 18 years of age.
- Be able to read and write the English language.
- Not have plead guilty or nolo contender to a felony or been convicted of a felony.
- Not have had a Notary Public commission revoked during the past five years.

NEW YORK
APPLICANT MUST:

- Be a citizen of the United States, and either a resident of the State of New York, or have an office or place of business in the State of New York.
- Have good moral character.
- Have the equivalent of a common school education.
- Be familiar with the duties and responsibilities of a Notary Public.
- Not have been convicted, in this State or any other State or territory, of a felony of the following offenses listed in the Notary Public License Law Handbook.

NORTH CAROLINA
APPLICANT MUST:

- Be at least 18 years of age or legally emancipated.
- Reside or have a regular place of work or business in this State.

- Reside legally in the United States.
- Speak, read, and write the English language.
- Possess a high school diploma or equivalent.
- Pass a course of instruction, unless the person is a licensed member of the North Carolina State Bar.
- Purchase and keep as a reference the most recent manual approved by the Secretary that describes the duties and authority of a Notary Public.
- Submit an application containing no significant misstatement or omission of fact.

NORTH DAKOTA
APPLICANT MUST:
- Be at least 18 years of age.
- Be a citizen or permanent legal resident of the United States.
- Be a resident of North Dakota, have a place of employment or practice in North Dakota or reside in a county that borders North Dakota and which is in a State that extends reciprocity to a Notary Public who resides in a border county of North Dakota.
- Be able to read and write in English.

OHIO
APPLICANT MUST:
- Contact the county in which you reside in (each county has a slightly different process).

OKLAHOMA
APPLICANT MUST:

- Be at least 18 years of age or older.
- Be a citizen of the United States.
- Be employed within Oklahoma or a legal resident of this State.

OREGON
APPLICANT MUST:

- Be 18 years of age or older at the time of appointment.
- Be a resident of this State at the time of appointment, or be a resident of an adjacent State and be regularly employed or carry on a trade or business within this State at the time of appointment.
- Be able to read and write the English language at the time of appointment.
- Be of good moral character.
- Not have had a Notary commission revoked for official misconduct during the five-year period preceding the date of application.
- Not have been convicted of a felony, or of a lesser offense incompatible with the duties of a Notary Public, during the 10-year period preceding the date of application.
- Have satisfactorily completed a written examination prescribed by the Secretary of State to determine the fitness of the person to exercise the functions of the office of Notary Public.
- Have satisfactorily completed a three-hour

Notary Public education course.

PENNSYLVANIA
APPLICANT MUST:
- Be at least 18 years old.
- Be a resident of or employed within the Commonwealth.
- Be of good character, integrity and ability.
- Have proof of completion of a three-hour pre-approved Notary Public course within six months preceding application.
- Not have been convicted of or pled guilty or nolo contendere to a felony or lessor offense incompatible with the duties of a Notary Public during the five year period preceding the date of application.
- Have not had a prior Notary Public commission revoked by the Commonwealth or any other state during the five-year period preceding the date of application.

RHODE ISLAND
APPLICANT MUST:
- Make a written application to the Governor over his or her own signature, stating that he or she is a qualified elector who is an actual resident of the State of Rhode Island.

SOUTH CAROLINA
APPLICANT MUST:
- Be registered to vote in South Carolina thirty days prior to an election.

- Be a United States citizen.
- Be at least 18 years old on or before the next election.
- Be a resident of South Carolina, declaring a county and precinct.
- Not be under a court order declaring mental incompetence.
- Not be serving a term of imprisonment resulting from a conviction of a crime.
- Have never been convicted of a felony or offense against the election laws or if previously convicted, have served an entire sentence including probation or parole, or have received a pardon for the conviction.

SOUTH DAKOTA
APPLICANT MUST:
- Have residency in this State or reside in a county bordering South Dakota and the applicant's place of work or business are within the State of South Dakota.
- Not have been convicted of a felony.

TENNESSEE
APPLICANT MUST:
- Be at least 18 years of age.
- At the time of election, be a resident of or maintain a principal place of business in the county from which he or she is elected.
- Have never been removed from office as a Notary Public for official misconduct.
- Have never had a Notarial commission

revoked or suspended.
- Have never been found by a court to have engaged in the unauthorized practice of law.

TEXAS
APPLICANT MUST:
- Be a Texas resident.
- Be at least 18 years of age.
- Have not received a final conviction for crime involving moral turpitude or a felony.

UTAH
APPLICANT MUST:
- Be 18 years of age or older.
- Lawfully reside in this State 30 days immediately preceding the filing for a Notarial commission and maintain permanent residency.
- Be able to read, write, and understand English.
- Submit an application to the Lieutenant Governor containing no significant misstatement or omission of fact.
- Be a Utah resident or have permanent residency or have permanent resident status.
- Be endorsed by two residents of the State who are over the age of 18.
- Pass the exam.

VERMONT
APPLICANT MUST:
- Be appointed by the assistant Judges of the County Court of the County in which you

reside, unless you are an Ex-officio Notary Public.

VIRGINIA
APPLICANT MUST:
- Be at least 18 years old.
- Must be able to read and write the English language.
- Have never been convicted of a felony under the laws of the United State or this Commonwealth, or the laws of any other State, unless such person has been pardoned for such felony or has had his rights restored.
- Be regularly employed in the State and perform Notary services in connection with their employment if they are a non-resident (must surrender his or her commission when he/she ceases to be regularly employed in Virginia).

WASHINGTON
APPLICANT MUST:
- Be at least 18 years of age.
- Be able to read and write English.
- Live in Washington State, or live in Idaho or Oregon while employed regularly in Washington or doing business in Washington.
- Have a $10,000 surety bond from an insurance company or bonding company.

WEST VIRGINIA
APPLICANT MUST:
- Be 18 years of age.

- Be a resident or employee of the State.
- Have no felony convictions.
- Have had no Notary commission revoked in the last 10 years.
- Be endorsed by 3 qualified electors.
- Be able to read and write English.

WISCONSIN
APPLICANT MUST:
- Be a United States resident.
- Be 18 years of age or older.
- Have at least the equivalent of an eighth grade education.
- Be familiar with the duties and responsibilities of a Notary Public.
- Have demonstrated adherence to laws according to the Wisconsin statutes with regard to arrest, citations, and convictions.

WYOMING
APPLICANT MUST:
- Be 18 years of age.
- Be a resident of the State of Wyoming and the county from which you are submitting application.
- Be able to read and write the English language.
- Not have been convicted of a felony; unless the felony has been pardoned, reversed, annulled, and all rights have been restored.

State requirements may be outdated or incomplete. Always contact your Secretary of State directly for your states specific requirements

CHAPTER TWO

BECOMING A CERTIFIED SIGNING AGENT

CHAPTER 2
BECOMING A CERTIFIED SIGNING AGENT

Once you are a commissioned Notary Public, you may also want to extend your area of expertise by becoming a Certified Signing Agent. A Certified Signing Agent is specifically trained to facilitate Mortgage Closings.

A Certified Signing Agent has an advantage over other notaries. It is because of their certification that they are chosen first by Escrow Companies to conduct loan signings.

Every State has different requirements when it comes to a notary conducting loan signings. Some States do not allow notaries to conduct loan signings at all, some States require a notary to have special certification, and in States such as California, a notary does not have to have any certification other than a notary commission.

It is important to find out what your State requirements are when you are exploring your options as a notary.

Becoming a Certified Signing Agent will help you avoid lawsuits in the future and it will also help expand your clientele. Majority of companies prefer someone whom is experienced in handling loan documents to conduct signings for their company.

If you are a Real Estate Agent, Escrow Agent, or have experience with loan documents, the training may be an unnecessary task for you to pursue. However, if you have no experience with loan documents, this training is definitely for you.

Simply reading through loan documents before a signing is not enough if you have no idea what the purpose of the document is, or its importance. I guarantee, whenever you go to complete a loan signing, that the client will have a question or two.

Loan signings can be time consuming if you have to call the Mortgage Company for every question that arises during the signing. Plus, the Mortgage Company would prefer someone with experience in loan documents in order to avoid a situation where the client feels uneasy and uncertain about what he or she is signing.

The client is about to make an important life changing decision, and having someone who is confident and experienced, will help him or her feel at ease.

The worst thing you could ever do is lose the Mortgage Company's client due to your lack of knowledge. Taking a Certified Signing Agent course will not make you an expert in loan documents, but it will at least go over the basics.

You will gain more experience when you actually began completing loan signings.

Becoming a Certified Signing Agent can also be a very lucrative business, allowing you to complete loan signings for some Mortgage Lending, Title and Escrow Companies.

There are plenty of associations that offer the training to become a Certified Signing Agent. The training and coursework goes in-depth on the process of conducting loan signings. A good course will provide sample loan documents and training to help you understand the significance of the document. You can become certified through the National Notary Association, Notary Rotary, and other various associations that offer the specialized training and certification. However, keep in mind when choosing where to get your certification the reputation of the company, and which Lenders or Mortgage companies will accept certification from that association. You can also take the course through multiple associations to become certified.

When you take the course through an association, that association will add you to their Certified Signing Agent directory, which will help bring business your way. Different companies are registered through the different associations; therefore, it is often beneficial to be certified through more than one company.

Some associations offer a class and some offer a self-paced course. It is important to choose wisely which associations you join and get your certification through.

You can research the association and search for reviews regarding their courses. The most important thing is being able to feel confident when completing your first loan signing.

It is also a plus, to join an association that brings you the most business. An association that has great reviews, blogs for you to discuss topics with other notaries, and offers an abundant amount of training is a good association to join.

In order to be a successful Signing Agent, it is wise to become an expert in the field.

By the end of whichever course you take, you should be skilled in handling and notarizing loan documents.

As a Certified Signing Agent, you will be able to assist Title, Escrow and Mortgage companies in the closing of real estate transactions, in essence expanding your business.

If you choose not to complete the training through an association, you can always seek guidance from a Title or Escrow Company. Some Title Company's often offer free training to Real Estate Agents or those interested in understanding Loan Documents.

A closing packet can seem quite intimidating, especially if you are presenting it to a client who has tons of questions. The documents used in closings vary by state. It is imperative to know what documents are required in a Mortgage Transaction within your own State before completing a signing.

Please note that a Notary Public is never to give advice or explain a document during a loan signing. However, it is important to be familiar with the documents, in order to direct the client to the proper location that will answer his or her questions accordingly.

Some of the most important documents to get familiar with include the Closing Disclosure, Payment Letter To Borrower, the Note, Good Faith Estimate, The Search or Abstract of Title, the Notice of Right to Cancel and the Deed of Trust. I have also provided a list and a brief description of some of the loan documents that you may encounter during a loan signing.

LOAN DOCUMENT DESCRIPTIONS

BORROWERS AFFIDAVIT:

The borrower attests that they have not done anything to affect the title to property, that they are not the subject of divorce or bankruptcy proceedings, etc.

BORROWERS CERTIFICATION:

Document that states that the borrower(s) have applied for a mortgage loan from the "Lender", understand and agree that the lender has the right to the full loan review process, and fully understand that it is a Federal crime punishable by fine or imprisonment, or both, to knowingly make false statements when applying for this mortgage.

BORROWER INFORMATION:

This document is to be completed entirely by the borrower(s) and signed.

CLOSING DISCLOSURE:

Outlines the lender's disclosures to the borrower(s). It replaced the hud-1 and truth-in-lending-act. It is used for purchase, refinance, commercial and construction loans.

CLOSING INSTRUCTIONS:

This document contains instructions from the lender specifying certain loan requirements and conditions.

COMPLIANCE AGREEMENT:

The borrower agrees to cooperate with the Lender or Lender's Agent in correcting any loan documents that may contain clerical errors after the loan closes.

CONSUMER CHOICE DISCLOSURE:

This disclosure is provided to the borrower because they may have inquired about a lender-affiliated mortgage or escrow company. The lender is stating that any referrals were only suggestions and that the borrower is free to choose any company that he/she desired.

DEED OF TRUST:

Transfers ownership of the property.

EQUAL CREDIT OPPORTUNITY ACT (ECOA) DISCLOSURE:

Federal law requires creditors to make credit equally available without discrimination based on race, color, religion, national origin, age, sex, marital status or receipt of income from public assistance programs.

ESCROW ACCOUNT DISCLOSURE:

Account held by lender containing funds collected in conjunction with monthly mortgage payments. Also known as impounds, the funds in this account are held in trust by the lender on behalf of the borrower, and are used to pay expenses such as property taxes and homeowner's insurance.

ESCROW WAIVER AGREEMENT:

This document allows the lender to waive its right to require the borrower to establish an escrow impound account to pay for such things as real estate taxes or hazard insurance premiums.

FLOOD CERTIFICATION:

Federal law requires that you obtain flood insurance, if you obtain a mortgage, and your property is in a designated flood zone.

GOOD FAITH ESTIMATE:

Is an estimate of settlement charges and loan terms. It lists the loan amount, the loan term, and the interest rate.

LOAN APPLICATION/1003:

An initial statement of personal and financial information required to approve a loan provided by the borrower and necessary to initiate the approval process for a loan.

LOAN SERVICING DISCLOSURE:

The collection of mortgage payments from borrowers and related responsibilities (such as handling escrows for property tax and insurance, foreclosing on defaulted loans and remitting payments to investors). Will disclose whether the borrower's loan will be sold.

NOTE:

Is a document that allows the bank to foreclose on the property if the loan is not paid accordingly.

NOTICE OF RIGHT TO CANCEL:

Gives the borrower three business days to cancel the loan.

OCCUPANCY AND FINANCIAL STATUS AFFIDAVIT:

A buyer makes certain declarations related to the buyer's occupancy of the property.

PATRIOT ACT DISCLOSURE:

Is used to verify the identity of the borrower. Notary Signing Agent completes the document, signs and dates it.

PAYMENT LETTER TO BORROWER:

Breaks down monthly payments, which includes payments towards the principal, interest rates, insurance, taxes, and more.

PRIVACY DISCLOSURE:

States that the lender does not disclose any nonpublic information about the borrower to anyone, except as permitted by law.

REQUEST FOR COPY OR TRANSCRIPT OF TAX FORM (4506):

Allows lender to get a tax return transcript, verification that you did not file a federal tax return, form W-2 information, or a copy of a tax form.

REQUEST FOR TAXPAYER IDENTIFICATION NUMBER AND CERTIFICATION (W-9):

Allows lender to request and review tax return information from the borrower, and/or governmental agencies.

SEARCH OR ABSTRACT OF TITLE:

Provides the history of the property.

SIGNATURE AFFIDAVIT AND AKA STATEMENT:

A borrower discloses any other names under which he or she is or has been known as.

TAX AUTHORIZATION FORM:

This authorizes the lender to withhold monies from the borrower's monthly payment to pay their taxes and insurance.

* It is possible that not all documents listed will be found in every loan package. Also, all documents will not appear in a loan package in the same order. The Deed of Trust, Occupancy and Financial Status Affidavit, and the Compliance Agreement is amongst the few documents within a package that require notarization*

CHAPTER THREE

SETTING YOUR FEES

CHAPTER 3
SETTING YOUR FEES

When starting a Mobile Notary Service, it is important to take into account, the supplies you will need to have a successful business.

It is a good idea to invest in a good quality printer. A laser printer that is wireless, scans, faxes, and has two trays for both letter and legal-sized documents is a good choice.

As a mobile Notary Public, you will get calls from a lot of companies that will email you documents and require you to print them out at your own expense.

It is also a good idea to have a reliable cellular phone, so that you don't miss out on business opportunities. If you can afford it, Smartphone's are a good investment. IPhone's and Android's have the capability to print documents and emails directly from your phone, especially if you have a wireless printer. You can also download free apps to help keep your business organized.

For example, there is an app called Invoice ASAP, which is free and allows you to create invoices directly from your phone and email them to the company. You can also print a copy of the invoice to help you keep track of your transactions for income tax purposes.

Once the company has paid you for your services, the app allows you to mark the invoice as paid. This helps you keep track of what company's you are awaiting payment from and those you have already received payment.

The app also helps you keep track of the companies you have worked with in order to request future business from them.

Another benefit of a Smartphone is that you can receive a free credit card reader from various companies and receive credit card payments from your clients.

The credit card reader is free, but there is a fee charged to every transaction that you complete. You can inform your client that there is an extra charge for using a credit card or you can just deduct it from your basic notarial fees.

The benefit of having a credit card reader and an app coupled with your business account is that your money goes directly to your business account immediately.

Along with pens, printer, ink, paper, and a computer, it is important that you have a reliable car. There is nothing worse than missing out on a transaction because your car is not working.

It is also important to keep track of your gas mileage that you use driving to client's houses and while passing out your business cards.

The maximum that a Notary Public can charge per notarized signature is ten dollars in the State of California. However, as a Mobile Notary Service, you can charge for travel expenses, and more.

If you work with a Mortgage Company, you can charge a fee for document preparation, the cost of printing documents, scans and or faxbacks. You can either charge for gas mileage per mile or set a flat rate fee. You can charge for your time, for weekend signings or a separate fee for late night signings.

It is very important to check with your State to see their rules and regulations on the maximum fees you can charge for your services.

When setting your fees it is important to keep in mind all the business expenses you will occur. For example, you want to make enough money to keep ink in your printer, keep an adequate supply of paper, pens, paper clips, and extra money set outside just in case you need to replace your printer or your computer.

It is also a good idea to shop at one place for your notary supplies to receive the most discounts. For instance, if you shop at Staples, you can get a free rewards card, that rewards you for every dollar you spend.

You can also return your empty ink cartridges to Staples, and receive reward bucks.

It is also a good idea to collect coupons and bargain shop to reduce the amount of money you spend on your supplies.

Supplies are not the only thing you need to set money aside for. Your appearance is also a part of your business success. It is important to invest in a professional wardrobe, keep your nails manicured, and keep your hair well kept.

Investing a few dollars on your personal appearance will help your business succeed. Just remember to stay within a reasonable budget.

Once you have all your supplies to start your business, it is important to immediately come up with a budget and some goals.

It is important to know how much your expenses will be to keep a successful business afloat. You will need to know how many transactions you will need to complete a week, in order to pay for business expenses, to pay your personal bills, and to make a comfortable living.

If you have a budget written out and you stick to it, your business should continue to flourish. If you need to complete three transactions a week to maintain your budget, you know what to aim for.

A good thing is if one week you have more than three transactions, you can set aside the extra money in your savings for those weeks, when you wind up not reaching your quota or for unexpected expenses.

Once you have a set budget, set goals, and your expected income, you should come up with your fees.

It is a good idea to do your research to see what other mobile notary services in your area are charging. You don't want to set your fees too high or too low.

You can set your fees around the same range of other mobile notary companies in your area and offer special discounts and promotions in order to boost your clientele.

For example, you can offer discounts to active military personnel, repeat clients, or to clients that bring you referrals. You can have holiday specials or you can offer "buy one get one free" signature notarizations some months.

You don't want to go overboard on discounts if you cannot afford it, but it is important to have your business stick out from the rest.

You can go to yellowpages.com and search for other

notaries in your area and click on those that have a website and see if they have their fees listed are contact them directly to see if they would be interested in being your mentor.

It is also a good idea to find out how many mobile notaries there are in your area, in order to be aware of your competition.

Networking with other notaries or choosing a mentor in your area, is a good choice to see what advice they have to offer to help expand your business. However, you do not want to copy someone's idea. You just need to have a basic idea of what it takes to help your business become successful.

Another important tip in having a successful business is keeping track of your invoices. On your invoices, be certain to list what the fees were for notarizations, travel, and so forth.

CHAPTER FOUR

GENERATING
BUSINESS

CHAPTER 4
GENERATING BUSINESS

Once you have set your fees and received all your supplies you can began to generate business. It is a good idea to have professional business cards with your cellular phone number and your website address.

Once you have your business cards you can take them to local Real Estate Offices, Law Firms, Title Companies, Lenders, Banks, and Escrow Companies.

You can also take your business cards to local Hospitals, Convalescent Homes, Nursing Homes, Jails and Bail Bond Offices.

It is important to disperse your business cards to as many businesses throughout your city as possible.

You also want to stay in contact with local companies in your area to make sure they don't run out of your business cards.

You should also sign up with as many associations as possible. When you sign up with an association, your contact information is added to a directory, so even companies that are in other City's or States have access to your business.

Also, most Mortgage, Title, and Escrow companies refer to association directories first to choose Notary Publics.

Some associations are free to join and some require a membership fee.

It is important to establish a good reputation with as many companies as you can, so you can get repeat business

You can also register with Signing Companies, who will outsource signings to your company. However, it is important to keep in mind that you are not an employee of the Signing Company; you are an Individual Contractor/Individual Business Owner.

You can download a list of signing companies off of Notary Rotary's website, which also have the companies ranked for your convenience, 5-star being the highest and 1-star being the lowest. You want to sign-up with as many 4 and 5-star companies as possible, because those are companies that your fellow notaries have ranked in regards to receiving payments on time, documents on time, and etc.

It is also a good idea to draft a professional letter, listing your services, and send it to as many companies as you can to let them know that you provide mobile notary services. You will also want to include a couple of business cards inside the letter. It is important to include your commission number, your certifications, all the associations you are a member of and anything that demonstrates your expertise as a mobile notary public.

A lot of companies close at five and would love to have a mobile notary on-call who is willing to work after hours.

You can also send a letter to your family and friends with a couple of your business cards enclosed. Within the letter it would be a good idea to inform them of your new business venture, and ask them to refer you to people they know who may need your services.

You want to stay relevant in people's minds. Whenever they need a notary public, or know someone else who may need one, you want your name to pop-up first in their mind.

It is also a good idea to invest in a name badge, a domain name and a website.

When out running errands within the community, if you are dressed professionally and have on a name badge, people cannot help but to look at the name badge to see where you work and what it is you do.

You can purchase an affordable name badge at mynamebadges.com. The name badge should simply display your name and the name of your company.

If by chance someone strikes up a conversation with you about your business it is a good idea to have your business cards on hand. On your business card it is a good idea to not only have your contact information but also your website address.

It is a good idea to purchase a domain name, using either your name or the name of your business. A domain name makes it easy for people to find you, it also displays to others that you are serious about your business.

Once you have a domain name you can set up a basic free website with vistaprint.com. It is a very simple process, even for those who are not computer savvy.

The first page of your website should list your services and should have a contact box. You want to make it easy for people to contact you, so don't make them search your website for your contact information.

You can list your fees somewhere on the second or third page, or if you want to keep it simple you could simply just create the first page only. If your fees fluctuate it may be a good idea to not list them and just ask people to contact you to request a quote.

It is very important that you list your credentials and association memberships on the first page.

Having a website, gives your business an even more professional appearance.

Your website should be connected to your email. It is important to have your email synced to your phone, so you can receive the email immediately. Once you receive an email from a potential client, it is important to call them within five minutes or less.

If a potential client cannot get in contact with you, they are going to go down the directory list and find the next notary public available.

You can go to yellowpages.com and yelp.com to add your business to their directories free of charge. You may also be contacted by someone from the company to see if you would like to pay a fee to have your name moved up on their directory list.

The same goes for Google and other browsers; you can pay a monthly fee to have your name pop-up on their search database.

It is wise to take advantage of as much free stuff as possible, before you start paying monthly fees to other advertising or marketing companies. You don't want to spend more money on marketing than you are generating.

Once you register your company and get a fictitious business name, you will start to receive letters from companies offering you products to help your business grow. It is important to do your research and to determine if what they are offering is really necessary for your business.

It is also important after every signing to send out a thank you card, thanking the company for choosing to do business with you.

In any letter you send out always include at least two of your business cards.

If you are doing extremely well in your business it is also a good idea to browse vistaprint.com and choose marketing pieces to help promote your company. You want to stay consistent in your marketing Material designs.

When completing transactions for some companies, the client does not take the time to remember your name; they assume that you work for the company. Leaving behind a business card with your company's name, gives them something to refer to when they are in need of a notary in the future.

You may also want to invest in a window decal, car magnets, or bumper stickers with the name of your business and contact number.

Car decals are a good investment when it comes to promoting your mobile notary company. When you're driving around town, you can be marketing your business at the same time.

It is also wise not to go overboard on marketing

supplies if you cannot afford to. You should always take advantage of free marketing tools first.

The most successful way to promote your business is by creating a functioning database with your client's information. You can use that database to store your clients' addresses in order to send them Christmas cards, Birthday cards, monthly newsletters, or marketing pieces to generate repeat business.

You can also contact your local Chamber of Commerce and attend networking events or get tips from them on how to promote your company within your community.

CHAPTER FIVE

MARKETING &
SOCIAL NETWORKS

CHAPTER 5
MARKETING & SOCIAL NETWORKS

Social Networks are free. They are also the fastest and most efficient way to reach a broad range of people and promote your company. You can use Facebook, Twitter, Instagram, Zillow, Trulia, and even LinkedIn to promote your company.

When you create a Facebook business page, you can direct your friends and family to "Like" your page and promote your company and services. When people "Like" your page a link will appear on their timeline letting their friends know that they "Liked" your business page and it will request their friends to "Like" your page as well. You will generate more "Likes" by posting useful material on your timeline that entices people to "Like" your post or leave comments. You can also "Boost" your post for a fee to expand its reach.

You should be posting to your business page daily. You can post question and answer post that generate feedback. You can post pictures relating to your company, flyers, marketing material. You can advertise your company's monthly discounts or offer a discount to people if they "Like" your page.

In the "About Section" of your page you should have a link to your company website, your contact information, and a list of services you provide.

It is very important to list what associations you are a member of and any special certifications you may have.

It also has a section for you to include your Company Overview and Mission Statement.

Your business card and or car magnet can have the Facebook logo directing people to "Like" your Facebook page. You want to get as many "Likes" as possible to reach as many people as possible. You can also create a Facebook ad to promote your page, which will increase your page visibility based on the audience you choose to target.

You can use Twitter to post tweets relevant to your signing experiences. This lets people know that you actively complete loan signings and you're experienced. With Twitter, it is easy to follow someone and inbox him or her requesting that they follow you back. You want to follow as many Mortgage Companies, Banks, Realtors, Title Representatives, and other Notaries as possible. Your target audience should be directed to those that will most likely be in need of your services in the near future. Your Twitter name should be your company's name. It should be used for business purposes only. Make sure that your Tweets, Re-Tweets, and images are professional at all times. Most importantly, make sure your Tweets are grammatically correct.

Realtors most commonly use Zillow and Trulia, and your goal is to target Realtors.

Realtors can refer you clients. When you set up your profile just put Notary Public or Certified Loan Signing Agent, instead of Realtor. You can also browse the site to find Open Houses and personally take your business card to the Realtor and ask to help them pass out their business card in return.

LinkedIn is a great sight to network with other professionals as well. You can list all of your qualifications, skills, and areas of expertise and people can endorse you. Your target audience should be Mortgage Brokers, Escrow Agents, Title Representatives, Realtors, and other people that will find your services of use.

Instagram can be used to post pictures of your marketing material and other promotional material.

It is very important that you do not post your clients name or personal information; you are obligated to protect your client's confidentiality.

All your Social Network accounts should be maintained daily, weekly, or monthly. They should all be used to refer people to your Business Website.

Every Social Network has a Help Section and some even offer Free Webinars. The Webinars not only show you how to use the network but also how to generate more Followers, Likes or Endorsements.

CHAPTER SIX

MARKETING YOURSELF AS A BRAND

CHAPTER 6
MARKETING YOURSELF AS A BRAND

The core to having a successful business is marketing yourself as a brand. You are your own personal brand. Your image, marketing material, and the manner in which you portray yourself during a transaction, is in essence your brand.

For example, Apple has branded itself to have the best products by promoting the fact that their products don't get viruses. As a result, consumers now view Apple as a trusted and reliable brand.

As a Notary Public, you want to be a trusted and reliable brand as well. If you take an appointment you want to show up on time and with all the necessary documents and supplies you need.

As a Notary Public, you want to create a brand that allows your clients the assurance that you are an expert and less prone to mistakes.

If you dress professional when going out to do a signing and you appear organized and knowledgeable, clients will not hesitate to write a good review on your behalf, or refer business your way.

It is important to know what you have to offer, and that you market your talents, accomplishments, and abilities accordingly.

If you have a website, list all the associations you belong to, your degree if you have one or credentials, and number of years of experience.

Even if you have a degree in psychology you still want to list whether you have a Bachelor's Degree or Master's Degree. You don't have to list the field or major, but you want to display to your clients that you are educated.

Clients often won't care what your degree is in, they just want to know that you are educated enough to help them understand the Loan Document process.

Also, if you have experience as a Realtor, Title, or Escrow Agent, you will want to list that on your website as well.

Having experience as a Realtor, Title or Escrow Agent also ensures clients that you are familiar with the signing of Loan Documents.

Listing all associations you are involved in allows clients to see that you are all about your business.

You want to list all certificates related to your Notary Company on your website as well.

Even if your Mobile Notary Company is not your main job, you still want to look like an expert in the field.

You may want to have a unique logo or slogan that represents your business. Just as Apple products have an Apple Icon on all their products, representing the Apple Company. You want to have a distinctive logo, slogan or Icon that represents your business.

Having a unique logo or slogan helps clients remember you. You can display your logo or slogan on your business cards, website, all marketing material, business receipts, and all other business pieces.

Marketing yourself as a brand and building brand recognition helps to set your business apart from the rest.

If you build enough clientele in your area, to where if anyone in your community is in need of a Notary Public, and you are the first to come to mind, than you are officially a notable brand.

In order to be successful you must set yourself apart from others. Be creative when it comes to building your clientele and marketing yourself as a brand.

Make sure everything you associate your business with, has a positive outlook.

As quickly as you build a positive brand, it can be damaged by client's reviews.

If you happen to have a bad signing experience, such as arriving late, it is important that you mend the situation.

It is important to first apologize. Respecting people's time should be your main priority. People don't want to spend their entire day looking over Loan Documents.

If you happen to show up late, don't make up excuses as to why you are late just apologize.

If the documents are not in order when you arrive to a signing, take a minute to fix the documents and apologize for the inconvenience.

If the client signs a document in the wrong spot, complete all other documents and arrange a plan to go print out the document and get it signed immediately. At least that way the client knows that when you return they don't have to waste more of their time, they will only have one document left to sign.

However, if you plan to arrive to every appointment ten or fifteen minutes early, even if there is traffic or unexpected delays, at least you will have an extra ten or fifteen minutes to spare.

Also, making it a habit of printing two copies of the documents allows you to have a backup document, just in case the client makes a mistake when signing.

You can add the cost of printing the two sets of documents to the company or client's tab. Let them know that your policy is to print a copy for the company and one for the client to keep. The company often prefers that you print two sets of documents anyway.

A part of being a reliable Notary Public is being prepared for the any and every situation that arises.

It is very important that before you embark on your career as a Mobile Notary, that you create a business plan.

The business plan should entail what your economical goal is for the year. It should entail how many signings you would like to have a week. Most importantly it should include a detailed marketing strategy.

You should know how you plan to generate business and receive referrals or repeat business.

It is important that you direct traffic to your website.

Also, once you start building your clientele, you can have clients post reviews on your website. Most importantly whatever description you have on your website about yourself make sure when you are actually in front of a client that you always display it.

Consistently marketing yourself as a brand keeps you current and relevant.

It is very important to network, build, maintain and nurture long lasting relationships with your clients and the companies you complete transactions for. Referrals and repeat business is what will set your business apart from the rest.

Become a familiar face within your local Title, Real Estate, and Escrow Companies.

Become an expert in signings by getting all the training and experience you can in order to stay current in your field.

Be a brand that is memorable and easy to find.

CHAPTER SEVEN

PROFESSIONALISM

CHAPTER 7
PROFESSIONALISM

Professionalism is a key factor in your success as a Mobile Notary Company. Since you are your own brand you must take on a professional appearance, mannerism, style and behavior.

Becoming a professional is making a lifestyle adjustment. It is something that requires practice. You should first start by creating a professional image that is suitable or appropriate for you.

You should always wear clean and appropriate clothing. If you are a woman it is important not to wear low cut shirts. You should practice good hygiene and grooming. You also don't want to wear strong cologne or perfume. Some people have sensitivity to fragrances, so you want to be mindful of them.

When determining a dress code that is appropriate for

you make sure it doesn't offend or distract your clients. Being a professional does not have to mean that you have to wear a suit and tie. You can wear a nice pair of clean jeans and a collar shirt or slacks.

If you are a woman I would avoid wearing dresses or skirts. Pants or jeans with a clean shirt are suitable for a woman entering stranger's homes.

Decide what is comfortable for you and what you think represents a professional.

After choosing professional attire, you want to work on having a professional demeanor. It is a good idea to practice punctuality and shaking hands when meeting a client.

It is also a good practice to look someone in the eye when talking to them. However, be aware of the fact that in some cultures looking someone in the eye is offensive.

It is important to keep the conversation business appropriate. Avoid making offensive or inappropriate jokes. Avoid engaging in conversation that makes your client uncomfortable.

A professional is aware of and respects people's ethnicity, religion, and culture. Most importantly a professional is an expert in their career field.

Be professional in the way you talk, write, dress, and act.

A professional learns every aspect of the job. A professional does not let mistakes slide by, and they admit when they make a mistake. Most importantly, a professional possesses knowledge, honesty, integrity, and they are reliable.

Being professional also means having the tools you need to successfully do your job. Arriving late to a signing and not having a pen, definitely does not display professionalism.

It is also important to always dress appropriately when in public, even when you're running personal errands. You never know when you will run into a past or potential client.

Practice professional etiquette in all that you do until it comes naturally.

It does not matter what you think about yourself, it matters how others perceive you.

As a Mobile Notary Company your car is your office, keep it clean and presentable. When you run errands around town and your attire is sloppy and your appearance is a mess, people will assume that your business attitude is the same way. They will assume that you are unorganized and unreliable.

You should wear attire that is decent enough to promote your business whenever the occasion arises.

CHAPTER EIGHT

STAYING
ORGANIZED

CHAPTER 8
STAYING ORGANIZED

It is very important to keep track of all your invoices from completed transactions, and receipts of supplies you purchased for your business, for income tax purposes.

Supplies can include pens, postage stamps, printers, paper, ink and anything purchased for your business within that tax year.

It is also a good idea to keep a gas mileage log, so you can be reimbursed for mileage on your car.

When filling out your Notary Public Journal it is important to fill it out completely, just in case you ever have to appear in court or if you are required to show proof of a notarization.

The most important key to having a successful Mobile

Notary Company is not only filling out your journal completely, but also keeping track of your invoices.

You want to make sure that you get paid for every transaction you complete. You should mark invoices that you have received payments for as paid and keep them separate from those that you are awaiting to receive payment for.

It is also a good idea to list the date that the company told you they would make the payment. If you have not received a payment by the date in which they gave you, it is okay to call and remind them or resend a copy of the invoice to them.

If you keep all of your invoices in order you will be prepared when its income tax time.

Plus, you can use the invoices as records and reminders of what companies are good to do business with. If you don't receive payment from a company or if it was a hassle receiving your payment, you may want to keep that in mind the next time that company requests your services.

You also want to have a contact management system. It is a good idea to have a hard copy of all your friends, family, past clients and company's you have done business with as well as one on your computer.

You should also send out weekly or monthly reminders to the people in your contact management system reminding them about your business.

You also want to have a place where you can take notes to write down things about your clients. For example, if you know your clients birthday, anniversary, kid's birthday, or other special dates, you can send them a birthday card with your name and your business logo or slogan included.

Plus, if one of your clients informs you that they may have a friend that will need your service, you would want to note that so you could contact them at a later date to follow-up.

Staying organized will not only help the expansion of your business, it will help you keep past clients coming back.

If your past clients continuously receive emails, cards or reminders of your business, you will remain fresh on their mind as their local Notary Public.

CHAPTER NINE

JOURNAL ENTRIES

CHAPTER 9
JOURNAL ENTRIES

It is important to see what your State requirements are for filling out your Notary Public Journal. Include as much information in your journal as possible for future reference.

It is important to always keep your journal in a locked and secure place.

It is also a good idea to purchase a Journal Privacy Guard to protect your client's confidentiality.

Make sure that the document requiring Notarization is completely filled-in before you notarize it. The person must sign the document in your presence.

A Notary Public cannot notarize documents for a spouse, parent, guardian, child, sibling, or an in-law.

JOURNAL TEMPLATE

The information in this chapter will be based off the journal template provided.

The first section on the left side ask for the "Notarization date and Time' which is the current date and time that the notarization is taking place.

Below that section is 'Date on document' and then reference number. For a loan signing, log the loan number as the reference number.

In the Fees box, include only the fee charged for the actual notarization. Do not include mileage fees or any other fees charged.

Next to the fee box, check the paid box once you have received your payment and include the date on which the payment was received.

In the second column on the left side titled 'Description of documents or proceeding' check all the documents that apply. If it is a loan signing check all the documents that are within your particular loan packet and in the blank space below that, include what type of Loan is being conducted, for example Refinance or Seller Packet. Also, write in this section if an acknowledgment or jurat was used.

In the third section on the left side in the section that reads 'additional information', this section is used to record any notes or details that you may need to remember later, such as if the person used their left thumb to provide a fingerprint instead of their right thumbprint and the reason being or etc.

The first column in the right side section that reads 'Signer Name and Address' copy the information needed for this section directly off the borrowers Identification Card verbatim.

In the second column on the right side titled 'Evidence of Identification' check the forms of Identification provided to you. Typically the most common form is a Driver License, which will be used as an example for completing this section. Check the box that reads 'Driver License' and then below that in the blank space, record the Driver License number, date of issuance, and the expiration date.

It is a good practice, that before you allow the person to sign their signature and provide their right thumbprint, to have them Affirm to an oath and give a verbal response as opposed to a head nod, that they understand and agree to what they are signing.

CHAPTER TEN

YOUR FIRST SIGNING

CHAPTER 10
YOUR FIRST SIGNING

A Loan Signing Agent is a Notary Public who guides someone through the signing of their loan-closing packet, insuring that the individual signs each document properly.

Loan Signing Agents are hired as an independent contractor to ensure that real estate loan documents are executed by the borrower, notarized and returned for processing on time.

In order to get Loan Signing appointments, you must sign up with as many Signing Companies as possible and list your company on as many notary directory lists as possible. For example, the National Notary Association, Notary Rotary, 123 Notary and Notary Café, just to name a few.

Also, pass out your business card to as many Real Estate offices, banks, Escrow Offices, Lenders and Title Companies as possible.

A list of signing companies can also be found on Notary Rotary and the NNA website. Contact the companies and sign up with them directly.

Prior to accepting a signing always discuss your fees with the company beforehand.

Once you accept a Loan Signing appointment, immediately contact the borrower and confirm the time, date, and location of the signing. It is also important to inform the borrower of the types of identification cards that he or she will need to present to you in order to complete the signing and verify that the identification card has the same name that will appear on the loan documents.

Some companies also require a photocopy of the borrower's identification card.

You may also be asked to collect funds from the borrower to cover closing cost and if that is the case, you just attach the check or money order to the front of the loan packet and ship it back with the documents as well.

If the borrower does not answer, never leave personal details on their voicemail. It is important to inform the borrower prior to the signing that you are a Notary Public and if they have any questions regarding the loan documents that they contact the Lender prior to the signing.

Never try to explain or go over loan documents with a borrower it could lead to legal issues.

Your job as a Notary Public is to simply verify that the person signing the loan documents is whom they say they are, and to insure the completion of the loan documents by the borrower.

Never print the loan documents until you have confirmed the appointment with the borrower. Once you have confirmed the appointment, print two copies of the loan documents, one for the borrower and one to send back to the company that assigned you.

If the borrower makes a mistake during the signing replace that document with the borrower's copy.

Always be respectful of people's time and arrive to a signing on time or call if you are going to be late. Show up to the appointment at least ten minutes early.

Confirm with the company prior to the signing, what color pen to use during the signing, and provide enough pens for all involved in the transaction.

Keep the documents to be signed neat and free of wrinkles and smudges.

Dress appropriate, business casual or professional attire is recommended for Loan Signing's.

Keep in mind that you are handling a great deal of the borrower's personal information and you want to have the appearance of a reliable and trustworthy person.

Once you are ready to begin the signing, place a copy of the documents in front of the borrower, and one in front of yourself. Inform the borrower that he or she can read through the documents as you go.

If possible have the borrower sit to the right of you, and the co-borrower to the right of the borrower, so that the loan documents can be passed around the table counter clockwise.

If the borrower has questions during the signing you can refer them to the document that will provide the answer to their question or call the loan company.

There are different types of loan packets from Seller Packets, Re-fi's to reverse mortgage. Seller's packets are typically small in size. However, the most common loan signing that you might complete will more than likely be re-fi.

Please note that a Notary Public is never to give advice or explain a document during a Loan Signing. However, it is important for the notary to be familiar with the documents, in order to direct the borrower to the proper document and section of a document that will answer all the borrower's questions.

After getting the table ready and receiving a copy of the borrower's identification, complete your Journal

Entry.

After completing the journal entry, complete an acknowledgement. These can be downloaded directly off the Secretary of State website if you live in California, free of charge.

The first document the borrower should look over is the Closing Disclosure, which outlines the Lender's disclosures to the borrower. Ask the borrower to ensure that the numbers are all correct before you begin signing the loan documents.

When presenting a document to the borrower, simply state the name of the document and inform the borrower where to sign.

If during the signing they have question about where their interest rate can be found or etc., direct them to the document that will answer their question accordingly.

Once the loan signing is complete, review all the documents for missing signatures, initials, dates, notary seal impressions, and etc. Leave your business card with the borrower(s) and thank them for their time.

It is important to keep the loan packet in the same stacking order once you receive them, do not change the stacking order from how it was received.

Contact the company that assigned you the signing and let them know that the signing has been completed, and give them the tracking number if necessary. When you ship the documents always get a receipt.

If the company requires the documents to be scanned or Fax-back there are cool apps that you can utilize on your mobile phone, such as CamScanner.

Send the company an invoice after the signing is completed. Try to provide as much information as possible on the invoice. Such as the loan number, property address and the borrower and co-borrower's name.

Many experienced notaries, often have to call the company, so don't feel like a rookie. The fact that you have the company's number on hand and appear organized is more than enough to demonstrate your professionalism.

The company will let you know when you can expect to receive your payment. Make sure you keep track of when you receive the payment. It is also important that you keep in contact with the company, requesting that they send more business your way.

If you remember nothing else, be confident and professional and your business will flourish.

-GOODLUCK-

SAMPLE
DOCUMENTS

SAMPLE LOAN DOCUMENTS

Closing Disclosure

This form is a statement of final loan terms and closing costs. Compare this document with your Loan Estimate.

Closing Information		Transaction Information		Loan Information	
Date Issued	4/15/2013	Borrower	Michael Jones and Mary Stone	Loan Term	30 years
Closing Date	4/15/2013		123 Anywhere Street	Purpose	Purchase
Disbursement Date	4/15/2013		Anytown, ST 12345	Product	Fixed Rate
Settlement Agent	Epsilon Title Co.	Seller	Steve Cole and Amy Doe		
File #	12-3456		321 Somewhere Drive	Loan Type	☒ Conventional ☐ FHA
Property	456 Somewhere Ave		Anytown, ST 12345		☐ VA ☐ ___
	Anytown, ST 12345	Lender	Ficus Bank	Loan ID #	123456789
Sale Price	$180,000			MIC #	000654321

Loan Terms

		Can this amount increase after closing?
Loan Amount	$162,000	NO
Interest Rate	3.875%	NO
Monthly Principal & Interest *See Projected Payments below for your Estimated Total Monthly Payment*	$761.78	NO
		Does the loan have these features?
Prepayment Penalty		YES • As high as $3,240 if you pay off the loan during the first 2 years
Balloon Payment		NO

Projected Payments

Payment Calculation	Years 1-7	Years 8-30
Principal & Interest	$761.78	$761.78
Mortgage Insurance	+ 82.35	+ —
Estimated Escrow *Amount can increase over time*	+ 206.13	+ 206.13
Estimated Total Monthly Payment	**$1,050.26**	**$967.91**

Estimated Taxes, Insurance & Assessments *Amount can increase over time* *See page 4 for details*	$356.13 a month	This estimate includes:	In escrow?
		☒ Property Taxes	YES
		☒ Homeowner's Insurance	YES
		☒ Other: Homeowner's Association Dues	NO
		See Escrow Account on page 4 for details. You must pay for other property costs separately.	

Costs at Closing

Closing Costs	$9,712.10	Includes $4,694.05 in Loan Costs + $5,018.05 in Other Costs – $0 in Lender Credits. See page 2 for details.
Cash to Close	$14,147.26	Includes Closing Costs. See Calculating Cash to Close on page 3 for details.

CLOSING DISCLOSURE

PAGE 1 OF 5 • LOAN ID # 123456789

Closing Cost Details

Loan Costs		Borrower-Paid		Seller-Paid		Paid by others
		At Closing	Before Closing	At Closing	Before Closing	
A. Origination Charges		$1,802.00				
0.25 % of Loan Amount (Points)		$405.00				
Application Fee		$300.00				
Underwriting Fee		$1,097.00				
B. Services Borrower Did Not Shop For		$236.55				$405.00
Appraisal Fee	to John Smith Appraisers Inc.					
Credit Report Fee	to Information Inc.		$29.80			
Flood Determination Fee	to Info Co.	$20.00				
Flood Monitoring Fee	to Info Co.	$31.75				
Tax Monitoring Fee	to Info Co.	$75.00				
Tax Status Research Fee	to Info Co.	$80.00				
C. Services Borrower Did Shop For		$2,655.50				
Pest Inspection Fee	to Pests Co.	$120.50				
Survey Fee	to Surveys Co.	$85.00				
Title - Insurance Binder	to Epsilon Title Co.	$650.00				
Title - Lender's Title Insurance	to Epsilon Title Co.	$500.00				
Title - Settlement Agent Fee	to Epsilon Title Co.	$500.00				
Title - Title Search	to Epsilon Title Co.	$800.00				
D. TOTAL LOAN COSTS (Borrower-Paid)		$4,694.25				
Loan Costs Subtotals (A + B + C)		$4,664.25	$29.80			

Other Costs		Borrower-Paid		Seller-Paid		Paid by others
E. Taxes and Other Government Fees		$85.00				
Recording Fees	Deed: $40.00 Mortgage: $45.00	$85.00				
Transfer Tax	to Any State			$950.00		
F. Prepaids		$2,120.80				
Homeowner's Insurance Premium (12 mo.) to Insurance Co.		$1,209.96				
Mortgage Insurance Premium (mo.)						
Prepaid Interest ($17.44 per day from 4/15/13 to 5/1/13)		$279.04				
Property Taxes (6 mo.) to Any County USA		$631.80				
G. Initial Escrow Payment at Closing		$412.25				
Homeowner's Insurance $100.83 per month for 2 mo.		$201.66				
Mortgage Insurance per month for mo.						
Property Taxes $105.30 per month for 2 mo.		$210.60				
Aggregate Adjustment		-0.01				
H. Other		$2,400.00				
HOA Capital Contribution	to HOA Acre Inc.	$500.00				
HOA Processing Fee	to HOA Acre Inc.	$150.00				
Home Inspection Fee	to Engineers Inc.	$750.00			$750.00	
Home Warranty Fee	to XYZ Warranty Inc.			$450.00		
Real Estate Commission	to Alpha Real Estate Broker			$5,700.00		
Real Estate Commission	to Omega Real Estate Broker			$5,700.00		
Title - Owner's Title Insurance (optional) to Epsilon Title Co.		$1,000.00				
I. TOTAL OTHER COSTS (Borrower-Paid)		$5,018.05				
Other Costs Subtotals (E + F + G + H)		$5,018.05				
J. TOTAL CLOSING COSTS (Borrower-Paid)		$9,712.30				
Closing Costs Subtotals (D + I)		$9,682.30	$29.80	$12,800.00	$750.00	$405.00
Lender Credits						

Calculating Cash to Close

Use this table to see what has changed from your Loan Estimate.

	Loan Estimate	Final	Did this change?
Total Closing Costs (J)	$8,054.00	$8,713.50	YES - See Total Loan Costs (D) and Total Other Costs (I)
Closing Costs Paid Before Closing	$0	-$29.80	YES - You paid these Closing Costs before closing
Closing Costs Financed (Paid from your Loan Amount)	$0	$0	NO
Down Payment/Funds from Borrower	$18,000.00	$18,000.00	NO
Deposit	$10,000.00	$10,000.00	NO
Funds for Borrower	$0	$0	NO
Seller Credits	$0	$2,500.00	YES - See Seller Credits in Section L
Adjustments and Other Credits	$0	$1,035.04	YES - See details in Sections K and L
Cash to Close	$16,054.00	$14,147.26	

Summaries of Transactions

Use this table to see a summary of your transactions.

BORROWER'S TRANSACTION

K. Due from Borrower at Closing	$189,762.30
Sale Price of Property	$180,000.00
Sale Price of Any Personal Property Included in Sale	
Closing Costs Paid at Closing (J)	$9,682.30
Adjustments	
Adjustments for Items Paid by Seller in Advance	
City/Town Taxes	to	
County Taxes	to	
Assessments	to	
HOA Dues	4/15/13 to 4/30/13	$80.00

L. Paid Already by or on Behalf of Borrower at Closing	$175,615.04
Deposit	$10,000.00
Loan Amount	$162,000.00
Existing Loan(s) Assumed or Taken Subject to	
Seller Credit	$2,500.00
Other Credits	
Rebate from Epsilon Title Co.	$750.00
Adjustments	
Adjustments for Items Unpaid by Seller	
City/Town Taxes	1/1/13 to 4/14/13	$365.04
County Taxes	to	
Assessments	to	

CALCULATION	
Total Due from Borrower at Closing (K)	$189,762.30
Total Paid Already by or on behalf of Borrower at Closing (L)	$175,615.04
Cash to Close ☒ From ☐ To Borrower	**$14,147.26**

SELLER'S TRANSACTION

M. Due to Seller at Closing	$180,080.00
Sale Price of Property	$180,000.00
Sale Price of Any Personal Property Included in Sale	
Adjustments for Items Paid by Seller in Advance	
City/Town Taxes	to	
County Taxes	to	
Assessments	to	
HOA Dues	4/15/13 to 4/30/13	$80.00

N. Due from Seller at Closing	$115,665.04
Excess Deposit	
Closing Costs Paid at Closing (J)	$12,800.00
Existing Loan(s) Assumed or Taken Subject to	
Payoff of First Mortgage Loan	$100,000.00
Payoff of Second Mortgage Loan	
Seller Credit	$2,500.00
Adjustments for Items Unpaid by Seller	
City/Town Taxes	1/1/13 to 4/14/13	$365.04
County Taxes	to	
Assessments	to	

CALCULATION	
Total Due to Seller at Closing (M)	$180,080.00
Total Due from Seller at Closing (N)	$115,665.04
Cash ☐ From ☒ To Seller	**$64,414.96**

Additional Information About This Loan

Assumption

If you sell or transfer this property to another person, your lender

☐ will allow, under certain conditions, this person to assume this loan on the original terms.

☒ will not allow assumption of this loan on the original terms.

Demand Feature

Your loan

☐ has a demand feature, which permits your lender to require early repayment of the loan. You should review your note for details.

☒ does not have a demand feature.

Late Payment

If your payment is more than 15 days late, your lender will charge a late fee of 5% of the monthly principal and interest payment.

Negative Amortization (Increase in Loan Amount)

Under your loan terms, you

☐ are scheduled to make monthly payments that do not pay all of the interest due that month. As a result, your loan amount will increase (negatively amortize), and your loan amount will likely become larger than your original loan amount. Increases in your loan amount lower the equity you have in this property.

☐ may have monthly payments that do not pay all of the interest due that month. If you do, your loan amount will increase (negatively amortize), and, as a result, your loan amount may become larger than your original loan amount. Increases in your loan amount lower the equity you have in this property.

☒ do not have a negative amortization feature.

Partial Payments

Your lender

☒ may accept payments that are less than the full amount due (partial payments) and apply them to your loan.

☐ may hold them in a separate account until you pay the rest of the payment, and then apply the full payment to your loan.

☐ does not accept any partial payments.

If this loan is sold, your new lender may have a different policy.

Security Interest

You are granting a security interest in
456 Somewhere Ave., Anytown, ST 12345

You may lose this property if you do not make your payments or satisfy other obligations for this loan.

Escrow Account

For now, your loan

☒ will have an escrow account (also called an "impound" or "trust" account) to pay the property costs listed below. Without an escrow account, you would pay them directly, possibly in one or two large payments a year. Your lender may be liable for penalties and interest for failing to make a payment.

Escrow		
Estimated Property Costs over Year 1	$2,473.56	Estimated total amount over year 1 for your escrowed property costs: Homeowner's Insurance Property Taxes
Non-Escrowed Property Costs over Year 1	$1,800.00	Estimated total amount over year 1 for your non-escrowed property costs: Homeowner's Association Dues You may have other property costs.
Initial Escrow Payment	$412.25	A cushion for the escrow account you pay at closing. See Section G on page 2.
Monthly Escrow Payment	$206.13	The amount included in your total monthly payment.

☐ will not have an escrow account because ☐ you declined it ☐ your lender does not offer one. You must directly pay your property costs, such as taxes and homeowner's insurance. Contact your lender to ask if your loan can have an escrow account.

No Escrow		
Estimated Property Costs over Year 1		Estimated total amount over year 1. You must pay these costs directly, possibly in one or two large payments a year.
Escrow Waiver Fee		

In the future,

Your property costs may change and, as a result, your escrow payment may change. You may be able to cancel your escrow account, but if you do, you must pay your property costs directly. If you fail to pay your property taxes, your state or local government may (1) impose fines and penalties or (2) place a tax lien on this property. If you fail to pay any of your property costs, your lender may (1) add the amounts to your loan balance, (2) add an escrow account to your loan, or (3) require you to pay for property insurance that the lender buys on your behalf, which likely would cost more and provide fewer benefits than what you could buy on your own.

114

Loan Calculations

Total of Payments. Total you will have paid after you make all payments of principal, interest, mortgage insurance, and loan costs, as scheduled. — $285,803.36

Finance Charge. The dollar amount the loan will cost you. — $118,830.27

Amount Financed. The loan amount available after paying your upfront finance charge. — $162,000.00

Annual Percentage Rate (APR). Your costs over the loan term expressed as a rate. This is not your interest rate. — 4.174%

Total Interest Percentage (TIP). The total amount of interest that you will pay over the loan term as a percentage of your loan amount. — 69.46%

Questions? If you have questions about the loan terms or costs on this form, use the contact information below. To get more information or make a complaint, contact the Consumer Financial Protection Bureau at

www.consumerfinance.gov/mortgage-closing

Other Disclosures

Appraisal
If the property was appraised for your loan, your lender is required to give you a copy at no additional cost at least 3 days before closing. If you have not yet received it, please contact your lender at the information listed below.

Contract Details
See your note and security instrument for information about
- what happens if you fail to make your payments,
- what is a default on the loan,
- situations in which your lender can require early repayment of the loan, and
- the rules for making payments before they are due.

Liability after Foreclosure
If your lender forecloses on this property and the foreclosure does not cover the amount of unpaid balance on this loan,

☒ state law may protect you from liability for the unpaid balance. If you refinance or take on any additional debt on this property, you may lose this protection and have to pay any debt remaining even after foreclosure. You may want to consult a lawyer for more information.

☐ state law does not protect you from liability for the unpaid balance.

Refinance
Refinancing this loan will depend on your future financial situation, the property value, and market conditions. You may not be able to refinance this loan.

Tax Deductions
If you borrow more than this property is worth, the interest on the loan amount above this property's fair market value is not deductible from your federal income taxes. You should consult a tax advisor for more information.

Contact Information

	Lender	Mortgage Broker	Real Estate Broker (B)	Real Estate Broker (S)	Settlement Agent
Name	Ficus Bank		Omega Real Estate Broker Inc.	Alpha Real Estate Broker Co.	Epsilon Title Co.
Address	4321 Random Blvd Somecity, ST 12340		789 Local Lane Sometown, ST 12345	987 Suburb Ct. Someplace, ST 12340	123 Commerce Pl. Somecity, ST 12344
NMLS ID					
ST License ID			Z765414	Z61456	Z61456
Contact	Joe Smith		Samuel Green	Joseph Cain	Sarah Arnold
Contact NMLS ID	12345				
Contact ST License ID			P16415	P51461	P71234
Email	joesmith@ ficusbank.com		sam@omegare.biz	joe@alphare.biz	sarah@ epsilontitle.com
Phone	123-456-7890		123-555-1717	123-555-7171	987-555-4321

Confirm Receipt

By signing, you are only confirming that you have received this form. You do not have to accept this loan because you have signed or received this form.

Applicant Signature	Date	Co-Applicant Signature	Date

Uniform Residential Loan Application

This application is designed to be completed by the applicant(s) with the Lender's assistance. Applicants should complete this form as "Borrower" or "Co-Borrower", as applicable. Co-Borrower information must also be provided (and the appropriate box checked) when ☐ the income or assets of a person other than the "Borrower" (including the Borrower's spouse) will be used as a basis for loan qualification or ☐ the income or assets of the Borrower's spouse or other person who has community property rights pursuant to state law will not be used as a basis for loan qualification, but his or her liabilities must be considered because the spouse or other person has community property rights pursuant to applicable law and Borrower resides in a community property state, the security property is located in a community property state, or the Borrower is relying on other property located in a community property state as a basis for repayment of the loan.

If this is an application for joint credit, Borrower and Co-Borrower each agree that we intend to apply for joint credit (sign below).

Borrower	Co-Borrower

I. TYPE OF MORTGAGE AND TERMS OF LOAN

Mortgage Applied for:	☐ VA ☐ FHA	☐ Conventional ☐ USDA Rural Housing Service	☐ Other (explain):	Agency Case Number	Lender Case Number
Amount $	Interest Rate %	No. of Months	Amortization Type:	☐ Fixed Rate ☐ GPM	☐ Other (explain): ☐ ARM (type):

II. PROPERTY INFORMATION AND PURPOSE OF LOAN

Subject Property Address (street, city, state, & ZIP)	No. of Units

Legal Description of Subject Property (attach description if necessary)	Year Built

Purpose of Loan	☐ Purchase ☐ Construction ☐ Refinance ☐ Construction-Permanent	☐ Other (explain):	Property will be: ☐ Primary Residence ☐ Secondary Residence ☐ Investment

Complete this line if construction or construction-permanent loan.

Year Lot Acquired	Original Cost $	Amount Existing Liens $	(a) Present Value of Lot $	(b) Cost of Improvements $	Total (a+b) $

Complete this line if this is a refinance loan.

Year Acquired	Original Cost $	Amount Existing Liens $	Purpose of Refinance	Describe Improvements ☐ made ☐ to be made Cost: $

Title will be held in what Name(s)	Manner in which Title will be held	Estate will be held in: ☐ Fee Simple ☐ Leasehold (show expiration date)

Source of Down Payment, Settlement Charges and/or Subordinate Financing (explain)	

III. BORROWER INFORMATION

Borrower	Co-Borrower

Borrower's Name (include Jr. or Sr. if applicable)	Co-Borrower's Name (include Jr. or Sr. if applicable)

Social Security Number	Home Phone (incl. area code)	DOB (mm/dd/yyyy)	Yrs. School	Social Security Number	Home Phone (incl. area code)	DOB (mm/dd/yyyy)	Yrs. School

☐ Married (includes registered domestic partners) ☐ Unmarried (includes single, divorced, widowed) ☐ Separated	Dependents (not listed by Co-Borrower) No. Ages	☐ Married (includes registered domestic partners) ☐ Unmarried (includes single, divorced, widowed) ☐ Separated	Dependents (not listed by Borrower) No. Ages

Present Address (street, city, state, ZIP/ country) ☐ Own ☐ Rent ___ No. Yrs.	Present Address (street, city, state, ZIP/ country) ☐ Own ☐ Rent ___ No. Yrs.

Mailing Address, if different from Present Address	Mailing Address, if different from Present Address

If residing at present address for less than two years, complete the following:

Former Address (street, city, state, ZIP) ☐ Own ☐ Rent ___ No. Yrs.	Former Address (street, city, state, ZIP) ☐ Own ☐ Rent ___ No. Yrs.

Former Address (street, city, state, ZIP) ☐ Own ☐ Rent ___ No. Yrs.	Former Address (street, city, state, ZIP) ☐ Own ☐ Rent ___ No. Yrs.

Uniform Residential Loan Application
Freddie Mac Form 65   7/05 (rev. 6/09)

Calyx Form - Loanapp1.frm (11/09)

Page 1

Borrower _____
Co-Borrower _____

Fannie Mae Form 1003   7/05 (rev. 6/09)

116

Recording Requested By:
TRISTAR FINANCIAL CORP.

And After Recording Return To:
TRISTAR FINANCIAL CORP.
1000 MAIN STREET
LOS ANGELES, CALIFORNIA 90025
Loan Number: 200911000

----------------- [Space Above This Line For Recording Data] -----------------

DEED OF TRUST

MIN: 1000000-0200911000-7

DEFINITIONS

Words used in multiple sections of this document are defined below and other words are defined in Sections 3, 11, 13, 18, 20 and 21. Certain rules regarding the usage of words used in this document are also provided in Section 16.

(A) "Security Instrument" means this document, which is dated   FEBRUARY 12, 2010   , together with all Riders to this document.
(B) "Borrower" is   RICHARD WILLIAM ROGERS, AN UNMARRIED MAN

Borrower is the trustor under this Security Instrument.
(C) "Lender" is TRISTAR FINANCIAL CORP.

Lender is a   CALIFORNIA CORPORATION   organized
and existing under the laws of   CALIFORNIA
Lender's address is   1000 MAIN STREET, LOS ANGELES, CALIFORNIA 91301

(D) "Trustee" is   FIRST TITLE COMPANY
412 EAST SIGNAL STREET, SUITE 409, LOS ANGELES, CALIFORNIA 90025

(E) "MERS" is Mortgage Electronic Registration Systems, Inc. MERS is a separate corporation that is acting solely as a nominee for Lender and Lender's successors and assigns. **MERS is the beneficiary under this Security Instrument.** MERS is organized and existing under the laws of Delaware, and has an address and telephone number of P.O. Box 2026, Flint, MI 48501-2026, tel. (888) 679-MERS.
(F) "Note" means the promissory note signed by Borrower and dated   FEBRUARY 12, 2010
The Note states that Borrower owes Lender   TWO HUNDRED TWO THOUSAND AND 00/100
                                    Dollars (U.S. $ 202,000.00   ) plus interest.

CALIFORNIA--Single Family--Fannie Mae/Freddie Mac UNIFORM INSTRUMENT - MERS
Form 3005 01/01   Page 1 of 14

117

Borrower has promised to pay this debt in regular Periodic Payments and to pay the debt in full not later than
MARCH 1, 2040

(G) **"Property"** means the property that is described below under the heading "Transfer of Rights in the Property."

(H) **"Loan"** means the debt evidenced by the Note, plus interest, any prepayment charges and late charges due under
the Note, and all sums due under this Security Instrument, plus interest.

(I) **"Riders"** means all Riders to this Security Instrument that are executed by Borrower. The following Riders are
to be executed by Borrower [check box as applicable]:

☐ Adjustable Rate Rider   ☐ Planned Unit Development Rider

☐ Balloon Rider   ☐ Biweekly Payment Rider

☐ 1-4 Family Rider   ☐ Second Home Rider

☒ Condominium Rider   ☐ Other(s) [specify]

(J) **"Applicable Law"** means all controlling applicable federal, state and local statutes, regulations, ordinances and
administrative rules and orders (that have the effect of law) as well as all applicable final, non-appealable judicial
opinions.

(K) **"Community Association Dues, Fees, and Assessments"** means all dues, fees, assessments and other charges
that are imposed on Borrower or the Property by a condominium association, homeowners association or similar
organization.

(L) **"Electronic Funds Transfer"** means any transfer of funds, other than a transaction originated by check, draft,
or similar paper instrument, which is initiated through an electronic terminal, telephonic instrument, computer, or
magnetic tape so as to order, instruct, or authorize a financial institution to debit or credit an account. Such term
includes, but is not limited to, point-of-sale transfers, automated teller machine transactions, transfers initiated by
telephone, wire transfers, and automated clearinghouse transfers.

(M) **"Escrow Items"** means those items that are described in Section 3.

(N) **"Miscellaneous Proceeds"** means any compensation, settlement, award of damages, or proceeds paid by any
third party (other than insurance proceeds paid under the coverages described in Section 5) for: (i) damage to, or
destruction of, the Property; (ii) condemnation or other taking of all or any part of the Property; (iii) conveyance in
lieu of condemnation; or (iv) misrepresentations of, or omissions as to, the value and/or condition of the Property.

(O) **"Mortgage Insurance"** means insurance protecting Lender against the nonpayment of, or default on, the Loan.

(P) **"Periodic Payment"** means the regularly scheduled amount due for (i) principal and interest under the Note,
plus (ii) any amounts under Section 3 of this Security Instrument.

(Q) **"RESPA"** means the Real Estate Settlement Procedures Act (12 U.S.C. §2601 et seq.) and its implementing
regulation, Regulation X (24 C.F.R. Part 3500), as they might be amended from time to time, or any additional or
successor legislation or regulation that governs the same subject matter. As used in this Security Instrument,
"RESPA" refers to all requirements and restrictions that are imposed in regard to a "federally related mortgage loan"
even if the Loan does not qualify as a "federally related mortgage loan" under RESPA.

(R) **"Successor in Interest of Borrower"** means any party that has taken title to the Property, whether or not that
party has assumed Borrower's obligations under the Note and/or this Security Instrument.

TRANSFER OF RIGHTS IN THE PROPERTY

The beneficiary of this Security Instrument is MERS (solely as nominee for Lender and Lender's successors and
assigns) and the successors and assigns of MERS. This Security Instrument secures to Lender: (i) the repayment of
the Loan, and all renewals, extensions and modifications of the Note; and (ii) the performance of Borrower's

covenants and agreements under this Security Instrument and the Note. For this purpose, Borrower irrevocably grants and conveys to Trustee, in trust, with power of sale, the following described property located in the

COUNTY	of	LOS ANGELES	:
[Type of Recording Jurisdiction]		[Name of Recording Jurisdiction]	

PARCEL 1: THAT PORTION OF LOT 1, OF TRACT NO. 4600, IN THE CITY OF LOS ANGELES, COUNTY OF LOS ANGELES, STATE OF CALIFORNIA, AS PER MAP RECORDED IN BOOK 1150 PAGE(S) 44 AND 45 OF MAPS, IN THE OFFICE OF THE COUNTY RECORDER OF SAID COUNTY, SHOWN AND DEFINED AS UNIT 13 ON THE CONDOMINIUM PLAN RECORDED ON JUNE 26, 1990 AS INSTRUMENT NO. 90-1136000, OFFICIAL RECORDS OF SAID COUNTY.
PARCEL 2: AN UNDIVIDED 1/40TH INTEREST IN AND TO LOT 1 OF SAID TRACT NO. 46000, EXCEPT THEREFROM THOSE PORTIONS SHOWN AND DEFINED AS UNITS 1 THROUGH 12, INCLUSIVE AND 14 THROUGH 41 INCLUSIVE.

A.P.N.: 2780-002-145

which currently has the address of   8624 OAKLAWN AVENUE, NO. 13 (CANOGA PARK AREA)
[Street]

LOS ANGELES	, California	91304	("Property Address"):
[City]		[Zip Code]	

TOGETHER WITH all the improvements now or hereafter erected on the property, and all easements, appurtenances, and fixtures now or hereafter a part of the property. All replacements and additions shall also be covered by this Security Instrument. All of the foregoing is referred to in this Security Instrument as the "Property." Borrower understands and agrees that MERS holds only legal title to the interests granted by Borrower in this Security Instrument, but, if necessary to comply with law or custom, MERS (as nominee for Lender and Lender's successors and assigns) has the right: to exercise any or all of those interests, including, but not limited to, the right to foreclose and sell the Property; and to take any action required of Lender including, but not limited to, releasing and canceling this Security Instrument.

BORROWER COVENANTS that Borrower is lawfully seised of the estate hereby conveyed and has the right to grant and convey the Property and that the Property is unencumbered, except for encumbrances of record. Borrower warrants and will defend generally the title to the Property against all claims and demands, subject to any encumbrances of record.

THIS SECURITY INSTRUMENT combines uniform covenants for national use and non-uniform covenants with limited variations by jurisdiction to constitute a uniform security instrument covering real property.

UNIFORM COVENANTS. Borrower and Lender covenant and agree as follows:

1. Payment of Principal, Interest, Escrow Items, Prepayment Charges, and Late Charges. Borrower shall pay when due the principal of, and interest on, the debt evidenced by the Note and any prepayment charges and late charges due under the Note. Borrower shall also pay funds for Escrow Items pursuant to Section 3. Payments due under the Note and this Security Instrument shall be made in U.S. currency. However, if any check or other instrument received by Lender as payment under the Note or this Security Instrument is returned to Lender unpaid, Lender may require that any or all subsequent payments due under the Note and this Security Instrument be made in one or more of the following forms, as selected by Lender: (a) cash; (b) money order; (c) certified check, bank check, treasurer's check or cashier's check, provided any such check is drawn upon an institution whose deposits are insured by a federal agency, instrumentality, or entity; or (d) Electronic Funds Transfer.

Payments are deemed received by Lender when received at the location designated in the Note or at such other location as may be designated by Lender in accordance with the notice provisions in Section 15. Lender may return any payment or partial payment if the payment or partial payments are insufficient to bring the Loan current. Lender may accept any payment or partial payment insufficient to bring the Loan current, without waiver of any rights hereunder or prejudice to its rights to refuse such payment or partial payments in the future, but Lender is not

BY SIGNING BELOW, Borrower accepts and agrees to the terms and covenants contained in this Security Instrument and in any Rider executed by Borrower and recorded with it.

The undersigned Borrower requests that a copy of any Notice of Default and any Notice of Sale under this Security Instrument be mailed to Borrower at the address set forth above.

_____ (Seal)   _____ (Seal)
RICHARD WILLIAM ROGERS   -Borrower   -Borrower

_____ (Seal)   _____ (Seal)
                         -Borrower   -Borrower

_____ (Seal)   _____ (Seal)
                         -Borrower   -Borrower

Witness: Witness:

_____   _____

CALIFORNIA--Single Family--Fannie Mae/Freddie Mac UNIFORM INSTRUMENT - MERS
Form 3005 01/01   Page 13 of 14

NOTE

_____, _____   _____,   _____
        [Date]   [City]   [State]

_____
                  [Property Address]

1. BORROWER'S PROMISE TO PAY

In return for a loan that I have received, I promise to pay U.S. $_____ (this amount is called "Principal"),
plus interest, to the order of the Lender. The Lender is _____
_____. I will make all payments
under this Note in the form of cash, check or money order.

I understand that the Lender may transfer this Note. The Lender or anyone who takes this Note by transfer and who is entitled
to receive payments under this Note is called the "Note Holder."

2. INTEREST

Interest will be charged on unpaid principal until the full amount of Principal has been paid. I will pay interest at a yearly rate
of _____%.

The interest rate required by this Section 2 is the rate I will pay both before and after any default described in Section 6(B) of
this Note.

3. PAYMENTS

(A) Time and Place of Payments

I will pay principal and interest by making a payment every month.

I will make my monthly payment on the _____ day of each month beginning on _____, _____. I will
make these payments every month until I have paid all of the principal and interest and any other charges described below that I
may owe under this Note. Each monthly payment will be applied as of its scheduled due date and will be applied to interest before
Principal. If, on _____, 20_____, I still owe amounts under this Note, I will pay those amounts in
full on that date, which is called the "Maturity Date."

I will make my monthly payments at _____
_____ or at a different place if required by the Note Holder.

(B) Amount of Monthly Payments

My monthly payment will be in the amount of U.S. $_____.

4. BORROWER'S RIGHT TO PREPAY

I have the right to make payments of Principal at any time before they are due. A payment of Principal only is known as a
"Prepayment." When I make a Prepayment, I will tell the Note Holder in writing that I am doing so. I may not designate a
payment as a Prepayment if I have not made all the monthly payments due under the Note.

I may make a full Prepayment or partial Prepayments without paying a Prepayment charge. The Note Holder will use my
Prepayments to reduce the amount of Principal that I owe under this Note. However, the Note Holder may apply my Prepayment
to the accrued and unpaid interest on the Prepayment amount, before applying my Prepayment to reduce the Principal amount of
the Note. If I make a partial Prepayment, there will be no changes in the due date or in the amount of my monthly payment unless
the Note Holder agrees in writing to those changes.

5. LOAN CHARGES

If a law, which applies to this loan and which sets maximum loan charges, is finally interpreted so that the interest or other
loan charges collected or to be collected in connection with this loan exceed the permitted limits, then: (a) any such loan charge
shall be reduced by the amount necessary to reduce the charge to the permitted limit; and (b) any sums already collected from me
which exceeded permitted limits will be refunded to me. The Note Holder may choose to make this refund by reducing the
Principal I owe under this Note or by making a direct payment to me. If a refund reduces Principal, the reduction will be treated as
a partial Prepayment.

6. BORROWER'S FAILURE TO PAY AS REQUIRED

(A) Late Charge for Overdue Payments

If the Note Holder has not received the full amount of any monthly payment by the end of _____ calendar days after the date it is due, I will pay a late charge to the Note Holder. The amount of the charge will be _____ % of my overdue payment of principal and interest. I will pay this late charge promptly but only once on each late payment.

(B) Default

If I do not pay the full amount of each monthly payment on the date it is due, I will be in default.

(C) Notice of Default

If I am in default, the Note Holder may send me a written notice telling me that if I do not pay the overdue amount by a certain date, the Note Holder may require me to pay immediately the full amount of Principal which has not been paid and all the interest that I owe on that amount. That date must be at least 30 days after the date on which the notice is mailed to me or delivered by other means.

(D) No Waiver By Note Holder

Even if, at a time when I am in default, the Note Holder does not require me to pay immediately in full as described above, the Note Holder will still have the right to do so if I am in default at a later time.

(E) Payment of Note Holder's Costs and Expenses

If the Note Holder has required me to pay immediately in full as described above, the Note Holder will have the right to be paid back by me for all of its costs and expenses in enforcing this Note to the extent not prohibited by applicable law. Those expenses include, for example, reasonable attorneys' fees.

7. GIVING OF NOTICES

Unless applicable law requires a different method, any notice that must be given to me under this Note will be given by delivering it or by mailing it by first class mail to me at the Property Address above or at a different address if I give the Note Holder a notice of my different address.

Any notice that must be given to the Note Holder under this Note will be given by delivering it or by mailing it by first class mail to the Note Holder at the address stated in Section 3(A) above or at a different address if I am given a notice of that different address.

8. OBLIGATIONS OF PERSONS UNDER THIS NOTE

If more than one person signs this Note, each person is fully and personally obligated to keep all of the promises made in this Note, including the promise to pay the full amount owed. Any person who is a guarantor, surety or endorser of this Note is also obligated to do these things. Any person who takes over these obligations, including the obligations of a guarantor, surety or endorser of this Note, is also obligated to keep all of the promises made in this Note. The Note Holder may enforce its rights under this Note against each person individually or against all of us together. This means that any one of us may be required to pay all of the amounts owed under this Note.

9. WAIVERS

I and any other person who has obligations under this Note waive the rights of Presentment and Notice of Dishonor. "Presentment" means the right to require the Note Holder to demand payment of amounts due. "Notice of Dishonor" means the right to require the Note Holder to give notice to other persons that amounts due have not been paid.

10. UNIFORM SECURED NOTE

This Note is a uniform instrument with limited variations in some jurisdictions. In addition to the protections given to the Note Holder under this Note, a Mortgage, Deed of Trust, or Security Deed (the "Security Instrument"), dated the same date as this Note, protects the Note Holder from possible losses which might result if I do not keep the promises which I make in this Note. That Security Instrument describes how and under what conditions I may be required to make immediate payment in full of all amounts I owe under this Note. Some of those conditions are described as follows:

> If all or any part of the Property or any Interest in the Property is sold or transferred (or if Borrower is not a natural person and a beneficial interest in Borrower is sold or transferred) without Lender's prior written consent, Lender may require immediate payment in full of all sums secured by this Security Instrument. However, this option shall not be exercised by Lender if such exercise is prohibited by Applicable Law.

If Lender exercises this option, Lender shall give Borrower notice of acceleration. The notice shall provide a period of not less than 30 days from the date the notice is given in accordance with Section 15 within which Borrower must pay all sums secured by this Security Instrument. If Borrower fails to pay these sums prior to the expiration of this period, Lender may invoke any remedies permitted by this Security Instrument without further notice or demand on Borrower.

WITNESS THE HAND(S) AND SEAL(S) OF THE UNDERSIGNED.

_____(Seal)
- Borrower

_____(Seal)
- Borrower

_____(Seal)
- Borrower

[Sign Original Only]

SIGNATURE AFFIDAVIT AND AKA STATEMENT

SIGNATURE AFFIDAVIT

I, RICHARD WILLIAM ROGERS
certify that this is my true and correct signature:

RICHARD WILLIAM ROGERS
Borrower   Sample Signature

AKA STATEMENT

I, RICHARD WILLIAM ROGERS
further certify that I am also known as:

RICHARD ROGERS
Name Variation (Print)   Sample Signature (Variation)

RICHARD WILLIAM ROGERS
Name Variation (Print)   Sample Signature (Variation)

RICHARD W. ROGERS
Name Variation (Print)   Sample Signature (Variation)

RICH ROGERS
Name Variation (Print)   Sample Signature (Variation)

RICH WILLIAM ROGERS
Name Variation (Print)   Sample Signature (Variation)

RICH W. ROGERS
Name Variation (Print)   Sample Signature (Variation)

Name Variation (Print)   Sample Signature (Variation)

State of CALIFORNIA

County of LOS ANGELES

Subscribed and sworn to (or affirmed) before me on this   day of
by RICHARD WILLIAM ROGERS

proved to me on the basis of satisfactory evidence to be the person(s) who appeared before me.

Signature

(seal)

124

NOTICE OF RIGHT TO CANCEL
(General)

Borrower:
Ronald Hollenbeck, Marjorie Hollenbeck

Loan Number: 1111652927890
Lender: **GTAC Mortgage Corporation**

Property Address: **1000 Amazola Arvenue**
               Torrance, CA 90501

Tax I.D. No.:

---

1. YOUR RIGHT TO CANCEL

You are entering into a transaction that will result in a lien on your home. You have a legal right under federal law to cancel this transaction, without cost, within three business days from whichever of the following events occurs last:

(1) the date of the transaction, which is the date the promissory note and mortgage or deed of trust are actually signed and acknowledged by you (you have indicated that this will occur on) **February 12, 2012** ; or
(2) the date you received your Truth in Lending disclosures; or
(3) the date you received this notice of your right to cancel.

Initial _____   Initial _____

Initial _____   Initial _____

If you cancel the transaction, the (mortgage/lien/security interest) is also cancelled. Within 20 calendar days after we receive your notice, we must take steps necessary to reflect the fact that the (mortgage/lien/security interest) (on/in) your home has been cancelled, and we must return to you any money or property you have given to us or to anyone else in connection with this transaction.

You may keep any money or property we have given you until we have done the things mentioned above, but you must then offer to return the money or property. If it is impractical or unfair for you to return the property, you must offer its reasonable value. You may offer to return the property at your home or at the location of the property. Money must be returned to the address below. If we do not take possession of the money or property within 20 calendar days of your offer, you may keep it without further obligation.

2. HOW TO CANCEL

If you decide to cancel this transaction, you may do so by notifying us in writing, at:

GTAC Mortgage Corporation, 3200 Park Center Dr. Suite 150, Costa Mesa, CA 92626
(creditor's name and business address)

You may use any written statement that is signed and dated by you and states your intention to cancel, and/or you may use this notice by dating and signing below. Keep one copy of this notice because it contains important information about your rights.

If you cancel by mail or telegram, you must send the notice no later than midnight of **February 15, 2012**
                                                             (date)

Initial _____   Initial _____

Initial _____   Initial _____

(or midnight of the third business day following the latest of the three events listed above). If you send or deliver your written notice to cancel some other way, it must be delivered to the above address no later than that time.

I WISH TO CANCEL
_____   _____
(Consumer's Signature)   (Date)

ON THE DATE LISTED ABOVE, I/WE THE UNDERSIGNED EACH RECEIVED TWO (2) COMPLETED COPIES OF THE NOTICE OF THE RIGHT TO CANCEL IN THE FORM PRESCRIBED BY LAW ADVISING ME/US OF MY/OUR RIGHT TO CANCEL THIS TRANSACTION.

Ronald Hollenbeck   Date   **Marjorie Hollenbeck**   Date

                                   Date   Date

Lender TRISTAR FINANCIAL CORP.

CUSTOMER IDENTIFICATION VERIFICATION
IMPORTANT INFORMATION ABOUT PROCEDURES FOR OPENING A NEW ACCOUNT

To help the government fight the funding of terrorism and money laundering activities, Federal law requires all financial institutions to obtain, verify, and record information that identifies each person who opens an account. What this means for you: When you open an account, we will ask for your name, address, date of birth, and other information that will allow us to identify you. We may also ask to see your driver's license or other identifying documents.

INSTRUCTIONS TO INDIVIDUAL COMPLETING THIS VERIFICATION

The named individual must present at least two (2) forms of identifying documents for review; at least one (1) of the identifying documents must be a government-issued document bearing a photograph of the named individual. Other identifying documents not specifically listed below must, at a minimum, bear the individual's name. Examples of other acceptable identifying documents include: Current government-issued visa; Medicare card; student identification card; voter registration card; recent property tax or utility bill; most recent W-2 or signed federal or state tax returns; bank statements; and proof of car/house/renter's insurance coverage. Please contact the above-named Lender if you have any questions regarding the acceptability of any identifying document.

Borrower's Name: RICHARD WILLIAM ROGERS   Date of Birth: MARCH 22, 1956
[X] Residential or [ ] Business Address:* 8624 OAKLAWS AVENUE, NO. 13 (CANOGA PARK AREA) LOS ANGELES, CALIFORNIA 91304

Taxpayer Identification Number (SSN):** 000-00-0000

Identifying Documents	Place of Issuance	ID Number	Date of Birth	Issue/Expiration Date(s)	Photo?
[ ] State/Foreign Driver's License					[ ] Yes [ ] No
[ ] State/Foreign ID Card					[ ] Yes [ ] No
[ ] U.S./Foreign Passport					[ ] Yes [ ] No
[ ] Military ID					[ ] Yes [ ] No
[ ] Resident Alien Card					[ ] Yes [ ] No
[ ] Social Security Card					
[ ] Birth Certificate					
[ ] Other:					[ ] Yes [ ] No
[ ] Other:					[ ] Yes [ ] No

ADDITIONAL COMMENTS
(e.g., please note any discrepancies in the borrower's identifying documents): _____

CERTIFICATION

I, the undersigned, hereby certify that: (i) I have personally examined the identifying documents indicated above presented to me by the named individual, (ii) I have accurately recorded the information appearing in the identifying documents I examined, and (iii) except as may be indicated above, each of the indicated identifying documents appears to be genuine, the information contained in the identifying documents is consistent in all respects with the information provided by the named individual, and, where applicable, the photograph appears to be that of the named individual.

Signature _____ Date _____

Name and Title _____

*For an individual without a residential or business address, provide an APO or FPO box number, or the residential or business address of next of kin or another contact person.
**For non-U.S. persons without a tax identification number, provide a passport number and country of issuance; an alien identification card number, or the number and country of issuance of any other government-issued document evidencing nationality or residence and bearing a photograph or similar safeguard.

SAMPLE INVOICES

COMPANY NAME
INVOICE

FROM:
[Name]
[Company Name]
[Street Address]
[City, ST ZIP Code]   INVOICE # 001
[Phone]   DATE:
00/00/000

TO: **FOR:**
[Name]   John Doe Mortgage
Refinance
[Company Name]
[Street Address]
[City, ST ZIP Code]
[Phone]

DESCRIPTION	AMOUNT
TOTAL	

Make all checks payable to **COMPANY NAME**
Payment is due within 30 days.

LETTER TO FRIENDS/FAMILY

Dear Friends and Family,

I hope you are doing well. This letter is to inform you about my new career change. I have started my own company called *name of company*. As a public officer, appointed by the Secretary of State, the sole purpose of a Notary Public is to be an official witness to the execution of important documents. It is the job of the Notary Public to verify and confirm the identity of the individual signing the documents. I specialize in Loan Documents, Mortgage Refinancing, Power of Attorneys, and more. I service the following counties *list counties.*

Whenever you or someone you know is in need of a Notary Public, I ask that you please call me first. Even if it's not in my county, I will research, and find you a Notary Public who is best suited to assist you. This is my profession and you are my family or friend and I want to help.

I've enclosed my business card with my updated information. Let me know if you think of anyone who could use my services. Also, don't hesitate to give me a call if you have any questions!

Talk to you soon,

Sincerely and Respectfully,

Your Name Here

LETTER TO LOCAL COMPANIES

INSERT
LOGO
HERE

Dear *Company Name*,

My name is *your name*, and I am your local Notary Public. I am also a Certified Signing Agent as well. I am available 24/7. I specialize in Loan Signings, I have experience with seller's packets, loan applications, refinances and more. I service the following counties as well *list counties.*

I am E&O insured and a member of the following associations *list associations*.

Whenever your company is in need of a Notary Public, I ask that you please call me first.

I've enclosed my business card with my updated information for your convenience!

Sincerely and Respectfully,

Your Name Here

YOUR COMPANY NAME HERE
Commission#

Office: 000.000.000
Cell Phone: 000.000.000
Your Company Website Address

ACKNOWLEDGMENT

ACKNOWLEDGMENT

A notary public or other officer completing this certificate verifies only the identity of the individual who signed the document to which this certificate is attached, and not the truthfulness, accuracy, or validity of that document.

State of California
County of _____)

On _____ before me, _____
(insert name and title of the officer)

personally appeared _____
who proved to me on the basis of satisfactory evidence to be the person(s) whose name(s) is/are subscribed to the within instrument and acknowledged to me that he/she/they executed the same in his/her/their authorized capacity(ies), and that by his/her/their signature(s) on the instrument the person(s), or the entity upon behalf of which the person(s) acted, executed the instrument.

I certify under PENALTY OF PERJURY under the laws of the State of California that the foregoing paragraph is true and correct.

WITNESS my hand and official seal.

Signature _____   **(Seal)**

JURAT

A notary public or other officer completing this
certificate verifies only the identity of the individual
who signed the document to which this certificate
is attached, and not the truthfulness, accuracy, or
validity of that document.

State of California
County of _____

Subscribed and sworn to (or affirmed) before me on this _____
day of _____, 20____, by _____
_____,
proved to me on the basis of satisfactory evidence to be the
person(s) who appeared before me.

(Seal)   Signature_____

CERTIFICATION OF POWER OF ATTORNEY

CERTIFICATION OF POWER OF ATTORNEY

State of _____

County of _____

I _____, Notary Public, certify that on _____, I examined the
   Name of Notary   Date

original power of attorney and the copy of the power of attorney. I further certify that the copy is a true

and correct copy of the original power of attorney.

_____
Signature of Notary

Stamp clear impression of notary seal above.

OPTIONAL INFORMATION

DESCRIPTION OF THE ATTACHED

_____
Title of Document

_____
Number of Pages

_____
Document Date

_____
Other Information

OATH TO WITNESS

1. "Do you solemnly state that the evidence you shall give in this issue (or matter) shall be the truth, the whole truth, and nothing but the truth, so help you God?"

-OR-

2. "Do you solemnly state, under penalty of perjury, that the evidence that you shall give in this issue (or matter) shall be the truth, the whole truth, and nothing but the truth?"

GLOSSARY OF TERMS

GLOSSARY OF TERMS

ACKNOWLEDGMENT:

Is the act of one who has executed an instrument in going before a Notary or other official authorized to take the acknowledgement and declaring that they have executed the document.

AFFIANT:

The person who is making the affidavit.

AFFIDAVIT:

Is simply a written statement sworn to before an officer authorized to administer an oath.

AFFIRMATION:

The act or an instance of affirming; state of being affirmed.

ATTORNEY IN FACT:

A person, not necessarily an attorney, who is given authority by means of Power of Attorney to sign or act on behalf of another individual.

CERTIFICATE OF ACKNOWLEDGMENT:

The certificate of a Notary Public, Justice of Peace, or other authorized Officer, attached to a deed, mortgage, or other instrument, setting forth that the parties thereto personally appeared before him on such a date and acknowledged the instrument to be a free and voluntary act and deed.

CERTIFIED COPIES OF POWER OF ATTORNEY:

A certifying person has examined the original document and the copy and attests that the copy is a true and correct duplicate of the original copy.

CERTIFIED NOTARY SIGNING AGENT:

Is a commissioned Notary with specialized training in Real Estate transactions.

CLOSING AGENT:

An individual who represents a buyer and handles the closing and the legal transfer of title and ownership from the seller to the buyer.

COUNTY RECORDER'S OFFICE:

The Recorder's office is the custodian of public records in its County, such as Real Estate transactions, Marriage records, and other documents.

FICTITIOUS BUSINESS NAME:

Is a legal trade name under which you can operate a business.

INDEPENDENT CONTRACTOR:

One that contracts to do work or perform a service for another and that retains total and free control over the means or methods used in doing the work or performing the service.

JURAT:

A Notary's certificate on an affidavit.

POWER OF ATTORNEY:
A document that gives an attorney in fact the authority to sign or act on behalf of another individual.

SECRETARY OF STATE:
The appointed or elected official in a State Government whose chief function is to distribute statutes, administer elections, keep archives, etc.

SIGNATURE BY MARK:
An x-mark made by a person in lieu of a signature.

SIGNING SERVICE COMPANIES:
Are companies that serve as the middleman between Closing Agents and Certified Notary Signing Agents in setting up Loan Document Signings.

SOLE PROPRIETOR:
Unincorporated business with one owner having all the net worth.

SUBSCRIBING WITNESS:
A person who attests the signature of a party to an instrument, and in testimony thereof subscribes his own name to the document.

NOTES

NOTES

NOTES

NOTES

NOTES

NOTES

NOTES

NOTES

ABOUT THE AUTHOR

Tyrina Quinn is Chief Executive Officer and Founder of Tyrina Quinn Mobile Notary Service.

As a successful Notary Public and former Realtor, Tyrina Quinn provides high quality Notary Public Services to Mortgage, Escrow and Title Companies, as well as to the General Public.

Tyrina Quinn has a Bachelor's Degree from Cal State University, of Long Beach. She is an experienced Notary Public and Certified Signing Agent. She is also an active member of the National Notary Association and attends workshops and meetings within her community, which allow her to network with other Realtor's, Mortgage Broker's, Lender's, and Title Representative's in order to stay informed and up-to-date with Loan Documents.

Tyrina Quinn's experience as a Realtor and a Notary Public led her to write this book.

ADDITIONAL RESOURCES

Tyrina Quinn Mobile Notary Service is a full-service notary company providing mobile notary services, online notary training courses and other notary resources!

To learn more about products and services offered by
Tyrina Quinn Mobile Notary Service

-OR-

VISIT:
WWW.TYRINAQUINN.COM

Made in United States
North Haven, CT
10 November 2023